A CYCLING ODYSSEY – SOUTHERN EUROPE

SHEILA AND PETER FINCH

MINERVA PRESS
MONTREUX LONDON WASHINGTON

ISBN 1 85863 511 X

First Published 1995 by
MINERVA PRESS
1, Cromwell Place
London SW7 2JE.

Printed in Great Britain by
B.W.D. Ltd., Northolt, Middlesex.

A CYCLING ODYSSEY – SOUTHERN EUROPE

Preface

Why would a middle-aged couple decide to leave their comfortable home and get 'on their bikes' to DO Europe? We can, out of the combination of circumstances, only surmise that the decision was not entirely ours. The opportunity was given to us, so it was up to us to act on it.

We had been cycling together for only three years but the serious planning had begun the previous summer. We had just returned from a wonderful (and for us, expensive) holiday in Cyprus to have Peter made redundant again. This was the second time in less than eighteen months and the signs for the same to happen to me were growing ever stronger.

"Well there won't be any more holidays like that again, so we'd better think of something DIY"
"Some people cycle round the world."
"Yes, but they're usually younger than us."
"How about circumnavigating the Med?"

A conversation on these lines took place one Sunday afternoon on a walk round the village after lunch. During the next few weeks we consulted our twenty year-old atlas and wrote to the Visa Centre in London from whom we found out that the process of obtaining visas for that route is most off-putting. We also thought a little more realistically about the prospect of cycling across North Africa and promptly progressed to 'Plan-B' - "How about following the wine regions along the north of the Med. instead? Where shall we go en route?" The latter question was to give the prospect some reality and from there it became a series of pilgrimages as well.

The first concrete decision was that we would start by catching the ferry from Plymouth (conveniently only fifteen miles away) to Santander in northern Spain. From there the obvious spot to head for would be Santiago de Compostella, a romantic sounding cathedral city which, as a place of pilgrimage, has featured in much of my historical reading over many years. Mainland Greece became the ultimate goal;

as we have holidayed in the Greek Islands a few times and liked what we had seen of the country, it seemed a good idea to visit the mainland also. Our plan, having taken root, began to grow: to follow the coast round the Iberian Peninsula, picking out some of the names of our favourite wines. So much of the planning was done with bottles lined up beside the map! Another thought which came to us was that we might be able to visit some of the places to which St Paul addressed his Epistles: Rome, Corinth, Thessaloniki and, if we could find it, Philippi. Once we had found it on a copy of an ancient Biblical map in the north-eastern part of Greece, that became the farthest point.

Peter's Preface

My Part:

I took it upon myself from the outset to get Sheila to Philippi no matter what, so I secretly planned finances to cover any problems that could arise, from the simplest to the most obscure.

The first thought was of our middle-aged bodies (I was forty-nine and Sheila forty-three at the outset). No matter how young we felt, would we be able to cope? Our bikes being second-hand, we would need to have enough money to replace them, or for car-hire, boat or plane fares, hotels etc. You may call this the easy way out but I called it forward planning.

Carrying almost £1200 in cash and traveller's cheques (our emergency reserve) between us; security was a major concern. I worked on the theory that the fewer people who knew about it (or us) the better. I applied this mostly when camping wild, choosing sites that were hidden from people and always from the roads. As the tent was olive green this was made easier, as the reader can imagine, but even then, on occasions, we pulled branches around us to make doubly sure of invisibility.

My part was also to tentatively push Sheila onward when the going got hard so that we could keep up to the daily target I'd set, it proved difficult sometimes. I would say that towards the end of the expedition there were times when I had difficulty in keeping up with her.

I must emphasise to the reader the importance of keeping to our schedule in order to reach our goal before the greater heat of the Mediterranean summer and all the extra problems that would bring.

I hope these few lines will explain some of what follows.

Chapter 1 Planning and Preparation

During the autumn we started collecting up-to-date maps and reading articles in newspapers concerning the countries we proposed to visit. We still had not mentioned the plan to anyone as we had no time scale as yet. We were tentatively thinking about leaving in the following September and hopefully arriving at the Mediterranean coast for the winter. Peter started working for himself in October operating his own business as painter/decorator/repair genius to establish something that could be left and picked up again on our return. With December came my eagerly awaited redundancy; it was such a relief no longer to have the threat of redundancy looming over me. (The atmosphere at work had become near to impossible and the redundancy gave us the spur, if we needed one, to decide if and when to go.) By tea-time on that Friday we had taken the plunge and set a date, Wednesday 24th March 1993, and within a few days had booked and had our passage confirmed – "No car, two bicycles".

At Christmas we told the family how we intended to spend much of 1993; the reactions ranged from disbelief to "Are you quite mad?" – We knew the answer to that one. However, they began to accept the idea; we had given them a hint as I had asked for "bike things" such as a dynamo for Christmas, and Peter had given me a bike-computer. Mum promptly bought me Anne Musto's book about her round-the-world-ride as an early birthday present, telling me I'd better go into print on our return.

With a target date set for departure, the remaining three months' training and preparation got under way to turn our very second-hand bicycles into precision touring machines and our bodies into enduring motors for them. Now that I was no longer tied to an office desk during the week, I set myself the task of cycling into one of the nearby towns at least twice and then three times a week. It was a sixteen mile round trip to be done whatever the weather. This became more comfortable after we had purchased our 'survival suits', specialised breathable cycling suits made of MVT material, which meant we stayed much drier and therefore warmer.

We had a great deal of equipment (or so it seemed at first) to collect, sort through and discard the surplus. Our intention was to be away for up to seven months, but the weight and space factor meant there was so much we could not take. Although we had information sheets on all the chosen countries from the CTC which told us where we could obtain certain spares, we still felt we had to carry most of what we might need. The unanswered question was, 'What can we afford to be without?' As our plan was to camp throughout, we would need to be completely self-sufficient. Where could we draw the line between essentials and have one or two little luxuries which could make life a bit more comfortable? As it turned out, neighbours were to help us with this last point. At our send-off party they presented us with a box marked "Essential travelling kit for cyclists touring the Continent". This contained (individually wrapped) all kinds of useful things from safety pins to Union Jack badges, foreign coins (labelled "For spending a penny abroad") to a miniature of brandy. This last item was broached on our final evening in Italy, when for the first time we had not been able to make the usual purchase of a litre of wine and we only had water and coffee.

We had to make several adjustments to our machines for touring, such as fitting pannier racks and most important, the standardising of our bikes to save on spares. The first task in this respect was to change Peter's 26" wheeled bike for another 27" one, as we thought this size was the same as continental wheels. We spent a great deal of time with Paul, our village bicycle dealer and repairman from whom we had made our purchases three years ago, collecting spares and picking his brains.

We had already bought some camping equipment when we had cycle-camped the Glastonbury Pilgrimage two years before, which lessened the amount we needed, but some things had to be improved upon. A set of lightweight pans with kettle replaced our heavy army-surplus pans and we added clip-together sets of cutlery; a double airbed replaced our two flimsy plastic ones and we bought one more king-sized pannier set which had a compartment for sleeping bags on the top. Once we had our panniers, (a king-size and pair of front ones each) we could decide what would fit in. The front sets were adapted from our original smaller back sets; I cut down the middle of the dividing panel and inserted an open-ended zip so that they could be used separately or as a pair (as for cabin baggage). Separately they could be attached to our front racks on either side of the front wheels. Peter built his front racks from various bits of aluminium and a barbag carrier we already had.

Lists of essentials were drawn up and then divided into how they could be packed. We would need to carry some of the smaller, heavier items in the fronts to ease the weight on the rear wheels. As our front panniers were low-riders, they could take quite a bit of weight before manoeuvrability would be affected. To this end we put most of the spares, freewheel, gear-changer and chain in there, otherwise the fronts would carry mainly clothing and food. As we progressed, we found we had to rationalise the packing, I found that one would take most of the spare clothes whilst the other was the larder. Peter's carried spare shoes, maps and tool kit as well as his clothes and spares.

We had to keep clothes to a minimum, though we later saw that the other cyclists we met had far more judging by their camp washing lines. In addition to what we set out in - trousers, long-sleeved T-shirts, sweaters, socks, underclothes and woollen gloves - we each carried:

2 pairs of shorts
2 T-shirts
swim things
2 spare underclothes
towel
track suit
wet-gear
sun hats
2 spare pairs of socks
2 blouses/shirts
sandals
thin rubber gloves[1]
dress clothes[2]
spare glasses
sunglasses

---

[1] The thin rubber gloves were for when it became very wet & cold and our woollen ones would have cooled us even more when wet. I do suffer from cold extremities, which turn white and painful, so these were quite a comfort.

[2] He carried a pair of non-crease slacks and a light sweater, whereas I had been treated to a length of polyester silk which I made into a suit. (It weighed all of three ounces and was packed scrunched up into a small plastic bag the same size as my bikini.) These were our 'best' outfits.

To go with our wet-gear cyclists' suits, I had made 'spats' from oilskin material which kept the worst of the rain off our shoes, which were just ordinary trainers, not expensive proper cycling shoes.

There was much discussion over the merits of cycling helmets; none of the countries we planned to visit made them compulsory so it was up to us to decide. We were sure it would be too hot to wear them for much of the journey. Would we really need them? Would they be a nuisance to carry? Peter had experienced some discomfort on one of our training runs. As we came up a hill, suddenly he slowed down and became very hot almost to the point of feeling faint. It was 50/50, I was in favour, he was against, but in the end they did come with us. In fact we had bought Peter's only a few weeks before the start of the expedition, though he had not at the time agreed to wear it. We did actually wear our helmets for 50% of the journey, only discarding them after it became impossibly hot, but even then we saw many racing cyclists wearing theirs. I was very glad of mine when I came off in a gully in northern Spain.

As regards repairs and maintenance, Peter had, a couple of years earlier, been given *Richard's Bicycle Book* which contains some very instructive chapters on how to get out of trouble. He spent many evenings with one or other bike in pieces on the dining-room floor proving to himself that he could get us out of trouble, changing and replacing any parts that might suffer. I think before this time he had never done anything more complicated than puncture repairs, but now we had bottom brackets disassembled (and put back again), hubs and bearings replaced and he fitted a dynamo and computer to each machine. The computers, at first seeming to be a luxury, proved very valuable during the training period and enabled us to keep a complete record, not only of speed and distance during the trip but interesting facts like maximum speed and average for each day (as well as the maximum speed on those downhill runs).

As both our bicycles were second-hand and of unknown age, many of the parts were worn, so Peter had the task of replacing several parts and teaching himself to do this whilst still in the comfort of home. Having access to Paul was a bonus and we made many trips to his workshop for advice and for the specialist tools we would need. For instance, when a new wheel was bought the freewheel and chain had to be changed so that meant we needed a freewheel-remover and a chain-link splitter. When we had to get the new freewheel, we made sure it was compatible as we discovered there are many sizes and fittings. When Peter changed a bottom crank, he found the bearings in a cage, but Paul talked him into putting bearings in loose but held in grease, thus he found that he could fit in an extra one. This proved a good idea, as the extra bearing means the crank can stand more loading and prolongs life. It also saves the potential hazard of a cage breaking up and causing real problems.

All this time we were adding to the tool kit which was becoming heavier by the day. There were so many different parts, needing so many different spanners. We had a ten-hole 'dog-bone' but needed at least ten other sizes, fortunately for some of these we found very lightweight ones and one other multi-size spanner. The heavy steel tyre levers were replaced by plastic ones which worked extremely well. One headache was trying to find a substitute for a large adjustable spanner needed for the headset and bottom crank; this was finally solved with a motor car oil filter remover (a short steel handle with a length of bike chain attached). Peter also had to make a spanner to undo the nut holding the crank to the axle, as no ordinary one would fit into the confined space. For this he used a cut down box-spanner ground very thin to fit. As it happened, we did find some tools and spares for sale in some supermarkets but we could not be certain of their compatibility and of course they are never around when you have an emergency. We had to be prepared for anything to happen – anywhere.

Shortly before departure, we had read an article in a CTC magazine about wheels exploding. It can happen that when they get hot, (as on long downhill runs when the brakes are operated for a long time) the inner tube can explode and the more worn the rim, the more likely this is to happen. Examining my aluminium wheels, we decided the rear one was quite badly scored, having had the wrong brake blocks used previously, so a new wheel had to be purchased and the correct and more expensive 'grey' blocks to be used and carried. This also proved a wise decision as in the Spanish mountains Peter's steel wheel did explode – but more of that later. The last move was to borrow the pedals off our tandem as they were quite new, which meant they had new bearings and hopefully would not have to be taken apart.

Our tool kit consisted of:

dog-bone spanner
cone & lock-nut spanners
cut-down box-spanner
freewheel spanner
set of five spanners (4-14mm)
adjustable 'chain' spanner
allen key (for handlebars)
pliers
chain splitter
file
two tubes lithium waterproof grease
crank extractor
plastic tyre levers
puncture repair kit with extras
spoke spanner
three screwdrivers (one flat, one posidrive, one electrical)
cable ties
the indispensable Stanley blade!

and the spares:

three sets bearings (wheels & cranks)
chain
freewheel
rear derailleur
six sets brake blocks
four long brake cables
two short brake cables
one universal brake cable
six gear cables
small tub of oil with six drops molyslip
bulbs for dynamo lights
twelve spokes and nipples
four 'world tour' tyres
five inner tubes (was to be six but one was

used prior to departure)
two spindles (front & rear) with cones and nuts
Assortment of nuts, bolts & washers

All the tools fitted into the PVC bag I had made, the spares were not very evenly divided between us, but took up surprisingly little space. All these we decided were essential and once our tool kit was packed, we could see what space was left for other equipment.

As mentioned we already had our tent, a Litchfield Beaver 4, a four-man dome which I suppose is fairly heavy by cycle-camping standards but we did want enough space to accommodate the bikes inside if necessary. I adapted it for the warmer weather we expected to meet, by inserting a net-curtain window for extra ventilation (and to keep out mosquitoes). We also left behind the heavy bag into which it was packed using plastic carrier bags, inside the panniers with a lightweight nylon case for the poles to be tied to my frame. To make it easier to blow up the double airbed, we bought a small footpump which lasted until we were in France. We also settled on a few luxuries, a radio, a little make-up for me and three travelling-games, (scrabble, backgammon and mini-mastermind). Other than these I think everything else was a necessity, at least for our standard of camping. With more expenditure, we could have upgraded and lightened our equipment; self-inflating air mattresses apparently are much lighter than our standard airbed but much heavier on the wallet. We did, however, lighten some items, I bought a handbag-sized hairbrush and cut off most of the handle, we bought light aluminium plates which could double for cooking, and our new pan set had two pans which were used as soup or cereal bowls, as well as for heating food. Our cooker was the smallest Camping Gaz one, as we felt sure cartridges would be quite easy to obtain. The two-cup size aluminium kettle was the star of the show especially in the earlier and colder part of the trip, though we loved our reviving cup of tea wherever we were.

We managed to get in one practice pack about six weeks before departure, everything we had selected seemed to fit. The amount of clothing and equipment was carefully weighed; it came to 20lb each, and on top of this we would have to allow for each day's food and drink, which we estimated would add another 5lb each, a maximum of 25lb to be carried by each bike in addition to the rider. As it turned out, the unaccustomed exercise reduced each of our body-weights by about half this amount. Anything more than the basic list would have to be scrutinised very, very carefully. All the equipment was then stowed upstairs in a box labelled "Do not disturb".

Our final equipment list looked like this:-

Large back panniers holding sleeping bags with sheet inners (which to start with was used as a neck scarf to keep out the northern cold at night) and either the tent outer or tent inner (one each).

Between us we carried:

air bed (double)
spare gas
plates & cutlery
wash-up liquid
wash things
camera & films x 4
maps
cooker & lighter
gas lantern
games
pan set & kettle
melamine mugs
radio
laundry liquid
pan scourer & cloth
first-aid/medical kit
airbed pump
folding water-container
mini-torch
mending kit

The ever increasing collection of maps was carried in front as were Peter's shaver, the camera and the torch. This did in fact leave room for carrying some food and extra water. The wet-gear fitted into very small bags tied under the saddles. The extra tyres we folded and tied to our front pannier racks. Peter was concerned that folding the tyres into a figure eight might cause distortion, however it was the most practicable way to carry them, and when they were needed they seated into the rims quite satisfactorily.

The only other factors in being away for an extended period was arranging for the house to be unoccupied; and the dog. Our dear old Jack Russell terrier had been getting more and more senile and frail over the past year; we had contemplated the idea of a neighbour having him to stay for the time we would be away but it seemed it would be difficult for such a long period. Just before Christmas we had been away for one night and he had been very confused, even to the point of disgracing himself on the hall carpet, and it became obvious he would not be able to cope. The decision had to be made, so, on the Monday before we were due to leave, I had to take him for his final walk to the vet. It was made even more difficult as our grand-daughter came over to tea that day; she is only four and devoted to all animals, but she seemed to accept that he was going for his 'Big Sleep' and then to doggy-heaven.

As my parents live in the other side of our semi, we had built in house-sitters, and they undertook to deal with utility bills and essential post. Insurance for the house and car was due for renewal, the car was to have a lay-up policy and the tax disc was returned for refund. We also bought a timing device for the electric lights, and for security we screwed up most of the windows and back door. In fact everything we could think of was done, gas and water turned off and not needed fuses removed, all at the last minute.

Another important question to be resolved was – how to carry money? Whenever we have holidayed abroad, we have taken traveller's cheques but this was to be longer than the standard two weeks and we expected to have to spend rather more than we usually take with us. Consultation with other travellers and with our bank manager, weighing up the merits of traveller's cheques, Eurocheques, Visa and currency, we settled on use of Visa backed up by traveller's cheques as a reserve, plus £200 worth of pesetas to cover us for the first few weeks in Spain. The bank manager assured us that Visa cards would be accepted in all our chosen countries and this proved to be an excellent method of drawing cash. Only a few times would the hole-in-the-wall machines not accept them with the instruction to "contact your bank", not very practical advice in the circumstances. This method meant we did not have to withdraw all the money needed at once, a great advantage.

Just about the only things left to prepare were ourselves. We had been cycling together for the three years since we bought our present second-hand bicycles; we started as a way to get fit and for local transport for ourselves without having to use the car. We discovered it to be so enjoyable that at the end of our first summer we did a weekend around Dartmoor with two nights camping. The following spring we cycled the Glastonbury Pilgrimage to celebrate my ten years of recovery from my stroke.

In 1981, whilst living in the USA, I had suffered a severe stroke brought on by overwork and the stress of living in a highly commercialised society. I had been unconscious for over a week and had had to hobble with a stick for several months having been left (initially) with a partially paralysed hip and a wobbly eye, the latter being corrected with surgery twelve months later. I had spent nearly three years getting to the stage when I could return to England and live on my own, some months before meeting Peter and later marrying him. It had been several years before I could walk without pain, and even now the stiffness still returns when I am very tired. However, I have found cycling very therapeutic, as is the sense of achievement it gives me. This was why Peter was so concerned with the making of contingency plans, as the furthest we had ever cycled before was the eighty miles to Glastonbury.

And there was the navigator's job; we had purchased maps of each country and now had to work out more exact routes and approximately measure distances. Using a borrowed map-measurer, we marked overnight stops (mostly at small villages) at approximately fifty kilometre intervals, making shorter daily distances in obviously mountainous areas. All along we had to remind ourselves that this was a proposed route and could be subject to change. On our previous overnight journeys we had taken everything with us, so we had little idea of how to transport our equipment. It was only one more step to strap larger panniers on and cycle away for six months or so, wasn't it? For the summer before I was made redundant, I was cycling the sixteen-mile round trip to work two or three times a week and some days Peter would come to meet me on the return, so we were getting in some mileage. We had set our sights on doing thirty miles a day, six days a week and we realised there was little chance of doing that during training. However, as Peter's work was all physical, I had to set about cycling as often as possible all through the winter. There were only a few times I could not get out three times a week. As 24th March approached, I managed to secure a temping job six and a half miles away; that was ideal as the car was now off the road; it meant regular travel and no excuses. For the final week we tried to get in thirty miles a day in the local area, which is hilly so it is hard work whatever the distance. In fact we were not far off our target on most of these days; the weather was kind and we had one or two nice picnics even though it was so early in the year. The thing we did not do was to go out with full panniers, as we decided that regular riding was more important.

One important factor, which we realised late in the training programme, was that we would encounter the problem of dehydration. We had felt very minor effects of this on foreign holidays before, but cycling every day would highlight it. Some years ago, when Peter was working inside a factory during very hot weather, he was issued with salt tablets. With these recollections in mind, we decided to seek advice. A local cycle shop proprietor told us of suffering dehydration abroad and having to be hospitalised; he advised a visit to the pharmacist. The latter told us that salt tablets were no longer available but we should put salt in our drinking bottles. This idea we found unacceptable so we made a firm rule to salt all our food and drink plenty of water even when we thought we were not thirsty. This always seemed to work; with hindsight we can see there were three occasions when this could have been the cause of my exhaustion, coupled with a sudden loss of enthusiasm which was quickly cured with rest and plenty to drink. We cannot emphasise enough the importance of this crippling condition to prospective adventurers.

On the final weekend before departure we had a party. Peter's sister came down from the Midlands and we invited most of our friends and neighbours. The map of Europe was displayed with the proposed route and we were given various names of places on or near to the route which our friends thought would be interesting to visit. Two of our friends gave us their holiday addresses in case we would be able to meet up, one in Portugal and one in Languedoc, France. We were also invited to a silver wedding party in September, "if you are back by then".

Chapter 2 To and Along the Costa Verde

After all the weeks of preparation, we could hardly wait to be off. Departure day dawned, 24th March, and our prayers for a fine day had been answered, no fear of getting drenched on the way to the ferry. We had asked Dick, a good friend, to drive us into the docks at Plymouth; although only fifteen miles away, we were concerned that if we had a puncture or a mechanical problem that would delay us we might be too late for the ferry and we could not afford to miss the boat.

At 8 am precisely, an embarkation party of parents and neighbours had gathered to see us off; at the time very few people knew we were only to cycle the half mile to Dick's house, but we did not feel we were deceiving anyone, we just did not want to start with an anti-climax.

Having set our computers to kilometres, we rode a full two that morning. Dick loaded us into his elderly Land-Rover, gave us sheepskins to cover the hard bench seats and we rode in style to the port. We could not help feeling a little strange as we waved good-bye to our friend. There we stood at the head of the queue for loading along with two motor-cyclists who thought we were really going to do it the hard way.

Travel in any form has always excited me and this was to be a first for us both. We felt like small children confronted by an enormous Christmas tree as we wheeled our bicycles into the great gaping mouth of the Bretagne. Our bikes were to travel in a special compartment with the motor-bikes on the car deck. We lashed them securely to the side rails before zipping together our front panniers to make cabin baggage and going up the many flights of stairs to find our lounge.

The Bretagne is one of the largest of the Brittany Ferries fleet, only having been in service for a couple of years. We found her very large and luxurious. As there were few passengers who had not booked cabin accommodation we were directed into Lounge 5, the Club Class Pullman lounge which normally attracts an extra charge. This is because the seats are wider and have extra footrests (and probably better padding). There was still half an hour to sailing time, so we went out on deck to watch the rest of the loading. Cars, motorvans, caravans and lorries were common-place but there was also a mobile home split in two and where was that Spitfire going to? Suddenly we saw two cyclists fully loaded like us wheeling aboard; we would have to try to find them later to swap notes! In the distance on the viewing platform, we could make out our friend Hilary who had come to see us off; she was shortly joined by Peter's son, daughter-in-law and grand-daughter, all waving frantically.

Suddenly everything started to happen, with winches whirring, the massive door began to close, the ship's horn sounded and the hawsers were gradually hauled in. We slowly started to move which prompted more vigorous waving, until we could barely see our send-off party. We turned to go down below putting England behind us to start the biggest adventure of our lives; our three months of planning and preparation were now to be put to the test.

Back down in the lounge, we found the other cyclists, a couple of Yorkshiremen living in Gloucestershire who were off to spend three weeks in Spain. They had cycled ninety miles the previous day (one with a broken spoke) in order to camp within easy reach of the ferry port. They told us they had little experience so far and had not decided on a definite route. We swapped training and technical experiences and told them of our plans before going off to explore the ferry. Once we had visited the bar and the duty-free and paper shops, we had over 23 hours of sea journey ahead of us. Much of this route is away from land but by mid-afternoon we passed Ushant. The north-west coast of France could be seen with its many towers, both water and navigation, surrounding the entrance to Brest harbour. On one of the decks was a display-chart with red lights showing our progress towards Spain, which we kept visiting impatiently. Crossing the Bay of Biscay was peaceful; just lazy swells rolling in from the Atlantic and not as the 'Bay' is so frequently portrayed.

After watching the sea for a while, the only things left to do were to eat and to sleep. The meals in the self-service restaurant were a bit on the lines of motorway services – fast-food and rather pricey, but nowhere else to go. However they tasted better than those we had eaten on the M5 and we made sure that we treated ourselves to a filling breakfast before leaving the next morning. I found my sleeping place rather less than ideal; the pullman seats, despite their comfort, are not so good if you like the luxury of sleeping horizontally as I do. So once we had bedded down, I spent a couple of hours dozing fitfully, before deciding that I would be better off on the floor; at least

I had a couple of blankets which softened the hardness very slightly. Maybe this was to be good training for the weeks ahead, when we had trouble with the airbed. At least it was more comfortable than the other ferry we took later in the expedition.

In fact we slept until about seven and we enjoyed the luxury of hot showers as, like our breakfast, we did not know when the next would be. Once again, the excitement made it difficult to while away the time, but it was not too long until we were entering Santander harbour and able to watch the docking procedure. Then we heard the broadcast to go below and retrieve our bicycles. It was quite crowded in the 'bike room' and as we strapped our front panniers back on we realised that redistributing the weights in them would have to wait; we had packed them with 'things wanted on the voyage' which would not usually be carried there, such as towels and wash things. It was a relief to get out, as the motor bikes, always in a hurry, were being revved up hard and spurting fumes and noise into the confined space we were sharing with them.

Out through the great mouth of the ferry and we were in Spain, just us and our bicycles with the whole of Europe ahead of us. No longer blasé and confident, we really felt quite small and vulnerable as we tried to get our bearings and start to find the way to Santillana. Although we had been to Santander seven years ago, it was perplexing trying to find the right road to Santillana. There were sign posts for larger places like Oviedo, but we were looking for minor roads and smaller places more suited, we thought, to our mode of travel.

Trying to find our way out of Santander was a bit of a headache. It was midday on a Thursday and the ferry had disgorged a large number of vehicles to join the already crowded streets of a busy port town. There we were in the middle of all this traffic, trying to remember to ride on the right and searching without success for signs to Santillana del Mar. In my halting phrase-book Spanish, I tried to ask an old man the way; I could not understand his voluble answer but the arm-waving and gesticulations were clear enough, or so we thought. Unfortunately, even though he may have told us it was a motorway, we did not realise until we approached our first set of "bicycles forbidden" signs; we were to see these too often in Spain and also in France, four categories of transport were not welcomed, the others being tractors, horses and pedestrians. So back to the junction and try again with all signs pointing to Santander. It was only by good fortune and navigation-by-nose that we found the correct road out into the countryside, peace, greenery and later signs to Santillana.

Santillana is a quaint old town and was just as we remembered it from our brief visit on our honeymoon. Narrow cobbled streets (for walking down not riding), stone and wooden carved doorways and shutters all bathed in the soft, sleepy afternoon sunlight that convinced us that we were now abroad. There were very few people but the one open shop supplied us with our first and most basic provisions, a loaf of bread and bottle of water. We stopped in the square outside Santillana's large church to take a photo and reminisce before heading out in the direction of Comillas, where we planned to stop for our first night. At 4pm we found a spot for lunch, the purchased bread with the cheese and fruit brought with us. We sat beside the road on the edge of a field and found it very relaxing, 'We will try to stick to quiet roads,' was the unspoken thought in both our minds at the time (and many others).

The road, though a minor one, was well surfaced and undulated westwards towards Comillas. It made a gentle introduction for us to Spanish roads. Just short of the town, we saw a campsite sign which pointed downhill to our left, to a lovely tree-surrounded site sheltering only a few caravans. There was a bar with several customers and a little shop which was opened up for us to buy supper. The weather had been very kind to us for our first day; we had ridden forty-seven kilometres in half a day and we had found a site open which had clean ablutions and warm showers. Contentedly we pitched our tent near to the limestone outcrops, away from the bar, and settled down to our first night under canvas (or rather nylon). We were the only campers and, as we felt new and nervous we brought the bikes into the tent with us.

The first few days on the Costa Verde were to begin to set the pattern for our travelling days. We quickly discovered that in this region and at this time of year, we should expect cool mornings, requiring gloves at the beginning of the day, even if it warmed up enough after lunch for shorts (as it sometimes did). On our first morning we saw the Picos mountains to the south of our road, a line of snow-capped peaks. We tried to establish a routine of clearing the site at 9am, pedalling for about two hours before a mid-morning break of tea and biscuits and continuing until 1.30, when we allowed ourselves not quite an hour for lunch. We would try to finish the day's cycling at about tea-time, an elastic time somewhere between 4 and 5.30. In this way we hoped to cover fifty kilometres a day but we had underestimated and on our first two full days clocked over ninety each day. It took several days before we began to shop more sensibly; we started by buying only enough in the mornings for our lunches, when we really needed to buy for the next twenty-four hours, as we could not always find a shop open in the afternoon. The siesta was universal, though not uniform in timing, and there was great variation in time of returning to work.

Our plan to keep to the coast meant we left the main road to La Coruna and joined the N634 at San Vincente, one of the stops recommended by Brittany Ferries, and headed for another, Llanes. Both are attractive fishing villages, though we passed through the outskirts rather than looking at them as sightseers would. This road is main enough to be well surfaced and had the disadvantage of being rather too well travelled but this was a factor to which we had to accustom ourselves. Many of these 'red' roads have hard shoulders, and where these were wide enough to cycle along, we felt grateful. The true Costa Verde is very picturesque, wild green and deserted, with alternating bays and dramatic dropping headlands. The fact that it was deserted gave us a problem on our second night when, in the late afternoon, we rode into our chosen campsite only to find it was not yet open for the season. Our map showed the next one to be at Ribadesella, a further ten kilometres along a more minor road.

This road had a much deteriorated surface, which punished bodies and bikes alike. The only facility in Ribadesella we could use was the Spar shop as once again we were faced with a closed campsite, so the only thing to do was look for a 'wild' site.

Our CTC notes informed us that wild camping was acceptable in Spain though permission from the owner should be sought where appropriate. In this case it was not, as the best place we could find was a quarry off the Gijon road. It was secluded and had been used partly as a dump, but not too recently. It seemed to fit perfectly into our specification i.e. remembering to look at it with the eyes of someone looking in rather than campers looking out. This was our basic rule which stood us in good stead for many, many more 'wilds' ahead. We found a flat place away from the fridges and rubble and attempted to put up the tent. The ground was much too stony to take any pegs, so the guy ropes had to be tied to boulders. We only saw one car all evening. Its occupants were almost certainly a courting couple, so they did not disturb us, even if they had seen our dark olive tent, which we doubted. We felt quite adventurous; only our second night and already we were camping wild and not being able to wash.

On the previous day, our first panorama had been the alpine-looking Picos and on the Saturday the road to Villaviciosa gave us views of the magnificent coastal scenery. Cliffs dropping dramatically into the sea, long river estuaries and pretty coves which we viewed from above. All this time we saw few people, except when we ventured into towns where we saw too many, mostly in cars. This first Saturday was an exception, as we were passed by large numbers of cyclists on racing bikes, looking as if they were in training for the Tour de France, which some of them probably were. They were a colourful and cheery crowd, waving and calling out greetings to us. We realised weekends must be their training days, as throughout our trip and in most countries we encountered cyclists either in groups or pairs. It was very cheering to see them, cyclists meant cycle shops should we need them later on and we did!

Gijon taught us a lesson we did not always heed, 'Towns and bicycles do not mix'. The signing in this town was for motorists only, preferably those who already knew the area. We found that the signs to Aviles, our next landmark, were only infrequent and then they pointed us once more to a motorway. We spent nearly one and a half hours just trying to find the right road. Eventually we asked a young man, who directed us through a tunnel and onto the right road, but what a road. It was the exit from the town but it ran through the middle of a power station. On one side of the road was coal, which covered us in black dust; on the other was red ash which made us look rusty as well as black. Of course the wind was blowing in circles at the time, so we emerged looking dreadful, how we looked forward to a campsite with a nice warm shower!

After Gijon, the road opened out and became rural and pleasant. Near Aviles we found a campsite sign but it stated that it was fourteen kilometres away. We had already clocked 90km and were rather tired. Again we looked for a wild site, and found the secluded corner of a field. Although there was a tractor driving up and down just over the hedge from us, we were not approached. We felt much in need of a restful night – however...

Our previous night in the stony quarry had, unbeknown to us, damaged the airbed causing slow punctures. Early the following morning, we awoke to find ourselves lying on the ground and this was to happen with disconcerting regularity over the next few weeks as we tried to locate and mend all the slow punctures. At the time of purchase, our airbed had been a bargain! For now we just pumped it up again and went back to sleep.

When we awoke at daybreak, it was to our first damp morning but we were glad of the damp grass initially as we had not been able to wash off the previous day's multi-coloured dust. The damp was not much more than drizzle but was enough to give us wet feet as we left our site. Aviles was an industrial rather than a pretty town, but was easy to navigate through. As we rode along, the drizzle ceased and near to San Esteban, we found sun, shelter from the headwinds and water to wash off the rest of the dust during our mid-morning break. This was beside a large estuary, where we watched rowing skiffs as we brewed up our tea. The town was on the distant hillside, hanging on for all it was worth. As it was Sunday and should have been a rest day, we were hoping for a short day's cycling. Declining the offer of a full bathe – it was still a bit cold – we mounted our bikes and went in search of a site. This we found at lunchtime, at La Playa San Pedro, near to Cabo Video.

It was a weekend retreat for the population of Oviedo, which explained why there were so many campers there. We found the ablution blocks rather primitive, being wooden sheds with outdoor basins and only cold water. Cold or not it was running water, so we were able to wash not only ourselves but our clothes. As it was a warm sunny afternoon, I was able to wash all the things that needed and get them almost dry, quite an achievement. Peter had his first introduction to stand-over toilets, good for washing the feet for the unwary, I could remember them from a holiday in France as a teenager, but if you have never seen then before they can give you a surprise.

It was also at this site that we had our first experience of eating out in Spain, since it was Sunday and the site had no shop, it was the only option for our evening meal. Obviously all the other occupants of the site knew more than us and had brought their own, as the fairly large restaurant was empty except for a group of young girls playing the fruit machine near the bar. We had fish and chips, served separately and packaged ice cream and it proved a very expensive meal. Even the bottled water was more than twice the price we had paid in the shops.

The following morning there was no-one stirring as we departed into the mist. The pillars of the soon-to-be-constructed viaduct for road improvements looked eerie through this mist. Even though we had diverted a few kilometres from our route, we agreed that the rest had been worth the extra distance; we felt more relaxed on a site and the water and wash had been well worthwhile. A few nights without washing ourselves did not make us very popular with each other, but we soon had to get used to it.

We decided that the N632 is a very pretty road, though a bit steep and windy. It gave us unparalleled views of the coast for the greater part of several days. After Canero, we rejoined the N634 and had to put up with more traffic, but at least we found that the lorry drivers tended to give us plenty of room. By lunchtime, it had become pleasantly warm, like a good summer's day at home, tempting us to strip off to T-shirts and shorts; it was easy to forget it was still March. Luarca was the main town that day, well sign-posted, and we came through it very easily and quickly. After Luarca the terrain evened out and we reached Navia very soon. Navia stands at the entrance to the river estuary of the same name, and just above the town is a large dam, one of three which provide water for a greater part of that area of Spain. At Navia, we saw a sign informing us there was a campsite only eleven kilometres away, but since we had been on a site the previous night, we were not so anxious to reach one and in fact found a lovely 'wild' far sooner. We were also uncertain as to whether these sites would be open, as our second day had taught us, so if a good 'wild' presented itself we would be in favour of it. We found this one down a lane about five hundred metres from the road, at the edge of a wood populated by red admiral butterflies. There were pine trees, gorse and willow branches on which to hang some of our still-damp laundry. All around us the sound of birdsong and, well in the distance, blasting and lorries, the sounds of a far-off quarry. Once that had stopped for the night, all was peace, broken only once, when after dark came a most alarming noise. I could only describe it as like a 'catherine wheel' firework going over the tent, Peter said it must have been a bird hunting, but I found it most alarming and was glad it did not happen again.

Tuesday morning started at 4 am when the lorries came to life. We also had to, as once again the airbed had deposited us on the ground, despite Peter's efforts with the repair kit. We tried to pump it up again and get a bit more sleep before it got light, but found we were to have a great deal of practice at this early morning exercise. When we awoke again, it was to a beautiful sunrise through the trees; fine mornings certainly encouraged us to be up and about.

Well before 9am, we had breakfasted and were on our way to Tapia de Cariego, where we found a good supermercado. As we had changed our route and decided to leave the coast road and head into the mountains for a short cut to Santiago, we had to stock up for a couple of days. The extra weight carried would probably be worth the extra effort, as the next sizeable town would be Lugo and if the mountains slowed us down as we expected, it could be a couple of days before we reached it.

We stopped for our mid-morning break before leaving the coast road and spent a little while in reflection; now on our sixth day we had already covered 350 kilometres. We had seen some really lovely scenery, we had not got lost, the weather had been kind and the bicycles performed very well. We felt quite confident in our ability to reach Greece, although there was still a very long way to go, but we had been well looked after and had been given an excellent start. We also felt satisfied, as we had ridden for six days consecutively without being too tired; we had never done more than two or three before, except during our final week of training and then the distances had been far shorter.

Chapter 3 Pilgrimage to Santiago

We had seen our first Camino sign, as we turned off the coast road onto the N640 towards Castropol. The Camino de Santiago is an ancient pilgrim route dating from, I believe, the middle ages, when pilgrimages to the shrine of St James were regularly made to atone for sins committed and to pray for miracles. The Camino proper runs through the mountains to the south of where we had travelled, but there is a branch of it which uses roughly the route we were now following. The Camino signs had all been repainted in blue and yellow to look extra smart, as 1993 was a 'Year of St James'. Whenever St James' day, 25th July, falls on a Sunday, the Spanish declare a 'Year of St. James' and Santiago celebrates. The first sign we saw was a walker's one, as it pointed off up a steep and narrow path but we decided to stick to the road and wait until we saw some more suitable looking ones. The route over the Sierra Meira was going to be steep enough without having to leave the road.

The valley of the Rio Eo started off climbing quite gently, but as it twisted and turned, 'Sod's Law of Cycling' began to apply. The wind always blows most strongly from the point to which you are trying to ride. The expedition scientist explained this as the wind funnelling down the valley off the mountains, but whichever way the wind was blowing, it was blowing and making our progress slower and the pedalling harder.

We had a lovely lunch stop that day, one of the prettiest. A rough track led steeply off the road down to the river where we sat on a sandy bank beside the water in the warm sunshine and washed our feet and socks. We basked contentedly in the sun and felt almost reluctant to move on to our over-eventful afternoon.

Our well-surfaced road was soon to become a construction site, the road disappearing beneath piles of dust and gravel. It seemed to us that whilst the new road was being built, on top of the old one, the old one remained open. For over three kilometres we were passed by heavy lorries, throwing up clouds of blinding, choking dust; diggers creating landslides alarmingly close to us and all the while the 'road' threatened to be swallowed up altogether, sometimes there were just a few posts to mark where we should ride. It was probably more dangerous than it appeared at the time. Due to the dust, we could hardly see where to go, we just knew the only way was onwards, so onwards we went. We were so relieved to reach the end of the roadworks and enter a town called Pontenova, which had the roughest main street we had yet encountered; we just hoped this would all change once the road was completed.

Once onto a smoother stretch of road, we felt confident of better progress but then the next problem hit us. Riding along side by side on the hard shoulder, a lorry came up behind us and we found ourselves too close together and unable to separate. Once our panniers touched, they locked together and steerage was lost, so the inside person (which was me) went over the edge into a storm drain. It was about three feet deep, very gravelly and with sloping sides. I was shown the wisdom of wearing my helmet as I had landed partly on my head as well as shoulder and thigh. What a lot of bruises and grazes! (We had changed into our shorts and T-shirts at lunch time). I was also rather shaken-up, especially when Peter pointed out how close I had landed to the point where the storm drain fell another eight feet into a large concrete hole. As my front wheel had twisted round completely, the brake yoke had snapped leaving me with only my back brake, which was not going to stop me on the mountainous roads ahead. Another lesson learned, cycling two abreast with panniers is a recipe for disaster!

Feeling sore and dispirited, all I wanted was a place to camp, which we were lucky enough to find within the next few hundred metres; our first streamside camp, a stretch of level bank shaded by trees and hidden from the road. The running water was most welcome to bathe my cuts and bruises while Peter swapped over our front brakes so I could have both whilst he managed by slowing the front wheel with his foot for the next couple of days. During the evening we saw an elderly couple looking down on us from their garden way above, but having satisfied their curiosity they went away for their supper. We also glimpsed another touring bicycle hidden away amongst the trees farther downstream, but we never saw its owner, so we passed another peaceful night with the ripple of the river running over the pebbles to lull us to sleep.

As we had decided to take the shorter road going over the mountains, we were to be confronted with mountain weather which was more severe than we ever expected. Maybe if we had researched more thoroughly we might have known what to expect, but we had chosen the most direct route to Santiago. We started off on what was a pleasant morning and within two kilometres glimpsed a pair of deer leaping off into the woods. As we climbed, the headwinds increased in ferocity and made the climb to the high pass at 575 metres really hard work. It took us much of the morning to reach this point on foot, pushing our heavily-loaded machines. Once we reached the top, we had the compensation of the ride down to Meira.

Meira, as well as being the mid-point of the Sierra, was a timber town. For the previous few days, many of the lorries which had passed us had been loaded with tree trunks and now we saw where they had been going. As we cycled through the town, the roads were lined with piles of logs and the whine of saws filled the air along with the pervading smell of sawdust. Further on we were to see signs for furniture-making and even further, timber-fired power stations. The sawdust was not the only smell we remarked upon at Meira, I found a bakery by following my nose. I bought a delicious loaf still warm though it cost me a bit more than previously, but made a good lunch and helped us fight the afternoon's headwinds. These winds of the Sierra Meira were very strong and at times dangerous, as when they blew from the side they threatened to have us off our bikes. Peter had previously had fears over the stability of my bike, which being a ladies model without crossbar was very unstable when fully laden. So much so, we discovered, that the back end would shake violently with just the slightest sideways movement of the handlebars, which meant in a strong crosswind it became a real handful. There were times that day when it shook violently and I had to take corrective action which fortunately was successful. Next time I am to have a hybrid or a man's bike.

The crosswinds never quite succeeded in knocking us off our bikes, as did a driver in Lugo, the next big town of the day. We had walked through the town in the rain and as we started to come out, felt that it would be safe to ride again, as the traffic had by then thinned out somewhat. We could see the way out of town, straight ahead with another road coming in to our right. Peter was leading, as the rain was making my glasses resemble a bathroom window. As I was pulling round a transit-type van parked on the hard shoulder, unbeknown to me there was a black car beyond inching his way out to see if all was clear. We did not see each other until the moment when we collided. He hit me on the right crank knocking me off and my pedal gouged out his indicator and parking lights. Fortunately, my foot was in the up position, which saved my leg from being hit and damaged. The first Peter realised was when I screamed and he turned round to see me on the ground with my bike shouting that I'd been hit, The driver leapt out and rushed over to help. Physically I was unhurt but my pride was very dented, and that was soon followed by shock.

Putting his bike down, Peter and the driver took my bike and I into a nearby car body workshop, which we think he may have owned. They sat me on a pile of tyres while they, and a couple of workmen examined my poor bike. The workmen set about it with a large lump hammer and started knocking the aluminium crank back into position – it made Peter cringe as he had visions of further damage being done. After this was completed and the back wheel could be spun he discovered the wheel was buckled. Peter threw up his arms in anger and despair and said to them "Santiago finished". I was not taking much notice as shock had set in, I was just a shivering, tearful heap sitting on my pile of tyres whilst Peter, armed with the phrase book and gesticulations was dealing with the situation. He was wondering if the whole trip would have to be abandoned but whilst the wheel was movable we were determined to give it a go. I think his words about Santiago must have done the trick as the driver then phoned a cycle shop to ascertain the cost of a new wheel and suggested to Peter that we should have it replaced and send him the bill. Imagining the problems this could entail, he gave the anglicised version of the Gallic shrug and emphatically said "No good". The message was received and seeing no other way we accepted his offer of the cost of the wheel, 7,000 pesetas (about £40). At least we had enough to replace the wheel in Santiago if need be. The cash was forthcoming and once we were back on the road, Peter had the thought "Was there some unwritten law that pilgrims to Santiago should be helped?", as it seemed the words had sparked off something that made them almost fall over backwards to get us on the road again.

As is the way when one falls off a horse, the essential thing to do is remount and get going again. I was forced to do this, although all I really wanted to do was to find a place to lay my weary and still (again) sore body. We discounted a conveniently placed but expensive looking hotel and opted to follow a sign indicating a hostel which never materialised. Once again onwards in the direction of Santiago, until we found a field that looked welcoming. I was so grateful to stop, and as the sky still looked threatening, we pitched the tent quickly for shelter with no chance of drying out. I was made to lie down for half an hour to recuperate while Peter made tea (unsweetened as thankfully we carried no sugar and I hate sweet tea). Could things get any worse?

It rained all through the night and it was so cold we kept our survival suits on, even inside our sleeping bags. Just about the only bad weather phenomenon we had not seen so far was snow...but as we struck camp the next morning the rain turned to sleet and then to snow. We had to set off walking and hope that either it would stop and melt, or we could walk out of it. After nearly an hour on foot, it eased off and turned to rain again. Once we had cleared the slush (which made for treacherous walking let alone riding) we were able to remount. How I had hoped some kind soul would stop and offer us a lift but it did not happen and it might have taken us out of the pilgrim classification.

It was on the following afternoon that we finally limped into Santiago de Compostella, after yet another night of camping wild, having cycled 569 kilometres with no outside assistance. Nine days of cycling, culminating in four days of mountain roads, diabolical weather and two accidents. As we neared the city, we saw more and more pilgrims. We had previously seen a few walkers but as we approached the city they were all along the road. All shapes and sizes of people, some carrying staves, most with backpacks and we even saw one lad with what looked like an enormous black bin liner over his shoulders resembling Frankenstein's monster. As we stopped for our elevenses, we were passed by a large party of schoolchildren, a noisy, cheerful and brightly coloured crowd they were. All, whether in large parties or smaller groups, were cheerful and gave us a wave or greeting, thus adding to the feeling of pilgrimage. Our excitement mounted as the first stage of the expedition neared completion. We were ecstatic as we found a campsite on the edge of the city. What luxury, an ablution block and no more need to 'go behind the hedge' for a few days, what did it matter that I could not get any hot water to start with? Just to have a shower after four days of riding increasingly further apart from each other was bliss.

Santiago de Compostella – so many of the towns on our chosen route had such romantic sounding names, and this one lived up to the image as far as I was concerned. The old city of St James, the martyr. The supposed last resting place of his bones, has been, at least, since mediaeval times, a city of pilgrimage. Pilgrims from all over the world still come for whatever reason and many nationalities were evident to us as we wandered the streets. From our elevated position on our campsite, we could see over the city into which we made our way by bus on the first afternoon of our stay. In fact it was only a short ride but what a contrast to be moving with someone else doing the driving and our legs not providing the motors.

On this Friday afternoon, the city was not too crowded and we were very torn between making first for the cathedral or finding a cycle shop to replace the broken brake parts. Having found a helpful young policewoman who directed us with clear instructions to the cycle shop, the brakes won. We had to buy a complete set, front and rear but at least now we would have a spare. We also looked for replacement wheels just in case, we even looked at replacement bicycles, fearing the worst. We also asked if they could repair my buckled wheel but the workshop would not be open again until the Monday as it was Palm Sunday weekend. Peter then felt forced into attempting to straighten the wheel himself using the instructions in the manual.

After we had done the essential shopping, we felt we could relax a bit and went in search of the cathedral, our main reason for coming. What an amazing building, very high, very dark and very imposing. We were lucky enough to arrive just in time to see the 'Swinging of the Censer' – a ceremony when eight monks haul on ropes to operate a ratchet mechanism which, having hauled the great silver censer up high into the centre of the cathedral, sets it swinging across the nave. At first it swung gently, arcing up towards the roof, but as it swung higher and higher, the speed of swing increased just like an adventurous child on a playground swingboat. At its peak, it was way up amongst the rafters, at least fifty feet above us, the coals of incense blazing in the silver bowl, then it rushed down towards us and away up the other side. I did not discover the significance of the ceremony other than to suppose it spread incense throughout the building very effectively. Later we were told the spreading of incense was to combat the pong before the days of deodorants! At least we had showered first. It certainly impressed us, as did the whole cathedral, especially the high altar. Richly ornamented in silver and gilt, it stood at least thirty feet high, beneath a gilded ceiling surrounded by candelabra and figures of angels. Of the churches and cathedrals we visited, this was probably the most impressive for its sheer size and magnificence but there were aspects of others that I liked better.

When we came out we went to buy postcards and it was when we found the post office for stamps that we made a surprising discovery. We only just reached it before closing time and there we saw, after more than a week, a public clock. We had been living on British Summer Time and had not put Peter's watch on when the Spanish had, so we had been an hour behind ever since arriving in this country!

The return journey to camp was quite difficult as we had quite a game finding the right bus. It involved leaping on and off several buses and showing the driver the map before finding one who confirmed that he was going to the right place. We had had a wonderful and productive afternoon and the rain had held off, although it was with us again for the evening and most of the next day.

We had decided to stay three nights at Santiago as we had the repairs to do on the bikes and we wanted to spend Palm Sunday in the city. Most of the Saturday was spent in bike repair and maintenance. In addition to the brake and wheel, we had our first puncture as we wheeled through the site gates and Peter's crank had developed a click. The great achievement was that he did a wonderful job on straightening my wheel with little more than the spoke spanner and the valuable pages of our manual. Following the directions and experimenting with the wheel, it returned to its original shape and stayed that way for the rest of the trip! Peter was amazed at how good the repair was, as he was not confident about being able to fix it, but he is always prepared to have a go first.

Later that afternoon we met our first fellow English travellers, a young couple called Sarah and Peter from Portsmouth who had been in Portugal and were on their way home. They had an old Volkswagen caravanette with a pair of mountain bikes. They said they had often found it easier to camp outside towns and use their bikes for sight-seeing. We were able to consult them about sites in Portugal and they told us of a good one at Caminha which we did use.

Palm Sunday and the rain had finally stopped, so we were able to spend the main part of the day in the city – far more crowded, but what an atmosphere. Tourist shops were doing good business as were the restaurants selling seafood and sustenance to weary pilgrims and tourists alike. We were not sure which category we fitted into that day. To start with, we were pilgrims as we joined a procession of palms into the cathedral. Palms woven into the most elaborate shapes joined with long plain palm branches and pieces of olive as they were all carried aloft to the sound of hymns and organ music. We stood in the nave entranced by the notes of the magnificent organ for quite a while watching the rest of the procession and watching the other pilgrims coming in. The congregation was such a mixture of people; pilgrims of all nationalities contrasted with the beautifully-dressed local children, for whose families it appeared to be a festival occasion; little girls in frilly white dresses stood next to those in walking boots and backpacks.

Once the sermons started (of which of course we could not understand a word), we went outside into the square and watched another procession. This time it was a figure of Christ on a donkey, being carried round accompanied by children dressed as Jewish people of the time and musicians in curious costumes which looked like Saracen dress; (this was lost on me as the Saracens of crusader times were far from Christian as well as being chronologically far from the time of Christ). It was a colourful and noisy procession and once it had passed and gone off into the streets, it was time for us to make our conversion into tourists. There was an Amnesty International parade in the park where we later had our picnic lunch and on all the street corners it seemed there were musicians. Best of these was a group of South Americans playing haunting pipe music and dressed in colourful costumes with big black hats. We resisted the temptation to buy souvenirs and by mid-afternoon our feet, unaccustomed to much walking, declared it was time to return to camp to read our English newspaper. After a scratch meal (it was Sunday and I had forgotten the food shops were not open) I phoned home for the first time from the site bar. Very expensive, I thought, six hundred pesetas for just a few minutes, but I felt pleased we had let them know all was well, and to hear that all was well at home too.

Our first rest period was almost over, it was back to being travellers and to prepare both mentally and logistically for the next stage, and whatever it would bring.

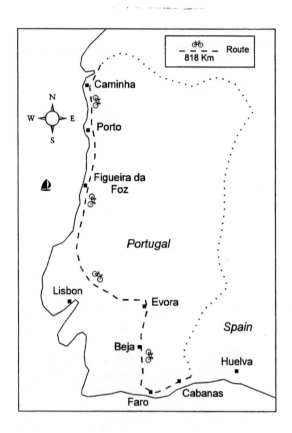

Chapter 4 Searching for the Sun (Portugal)

To be fair, Santiago is still in the mountainous part of Spain so we should not have been surprised that it was still cold; but nearly two weeks into our expedition we were really longing to find some warmth in which to camp. We left Santiago on yet another damp morning; however glad we were of our survival suits, we were looking forward to not needing to use them. Both our bicycles had benefited from their repair and resuscitation weekend, my wheel seemed perfect and I was quite used to the slight change of angle in the pedal crank; Peter's crank click had disappeared, as he had completely stripped the bearings, re-greased and replaced with new bearings and no cages.

As we reached lower ground, we began to see vineyards, in fact our last night in this part of Spain was spent alongside one where we were serenaded by a cuckoo. On the second morning after leaving Santiago we met the Portuguese border. The border crossing was by way of a long narrow bridge across the Rio Mino. As we approached, there was a great deal of traffic waiting to cross, so we made a rapid conversion into pedestrians and crossed by the footbridge – oh the convenience of being a cyclist! The border town of Valenca was all cobbled streets so we had to continue as pedestrians. Again our passports were not stamped, one of the advantages of being in the EEC, but I would have liked a record of our progress there also.

A new country meant new currency. Our Spanish money had lasted, so we had not yet had to use the Visa card to draw money, This was also thanks to our 'profit' from the accident as we had not had to use the £40 worth to replace the wheel after all. At Valenca the hole-in-the-wall would not co-operate, so we had to change a small traveller's cheque, in order to buy food to last until we could find a Visa machine that would deliver. Over our picnic lunch, we did a quick recap on Spain. We had spent five nights on sites and six wild and we had cycled 780 kilometres. We had spent an average of £7.50 each per day (at an exchange rate of about 160 pesetas/£) and that included the cost of one meal out and the bike parts (£10) so we were well within our budget.

Our first night in Portugal was at the site at Caminha that Sarah and Peter had told us of. At the far end of the town, adjacent to a beach and estuary across which we could see the white houses with red tiled roofs of a village, it was a lovely spot. We reached it at mid-afternoon whilst the sun was shining, warming our chilled bodies, so that after showering we could walk on the beach and pretend to be on holiday for a few hours. We had shopped for provisions in a small supermarket where the girl assistant spoke excellent English of which she was justly proud. In this shop we bought the cheapest Vinho Verde in a hefty glass bottle and our first bar of 'Tiger Soap'. The latter started off a clear amber lump of a rather evil-smelling substance but it was used thereafter to wash clothes and dishes, as it was the most convenient to carry. It did, however, turn a disgusting yellow after dampening and had the tendency to soften and adhere to everything in my pannier once it escaped from its plastic bag.

By the time we entered our second week we had settled into a routine. Physically we had settled down as our bodies had become used to the increased level of activity and we found that in Portugal we could cover well over fifty miles a day without any problems. This was helped by the terrain being flat though some of the roads were somewhat featureless on the way down to Porto, the only large city in the north of the country. We were still keeping to main roads as we wanted to get as far south as we could as quickly as possible, still searching for sun and warmth.

Well worth mentioning was the site we found on our second night, quite hidden away on the outskirts of Vila do Condo. We discovered it from the one sign pointing through the tiled houses towards what looked like a dead end. Peter described it as looking like the cottage owned by Little Red Riding Hood's grandmother, a tiny cottage surrounded by trees in a pine wood, where we disturbed a kindly old Frenchman. We had been advised that French was sometimes spoken in Portugal and I had been mentally preparing some phrases from my schoolgirl past. He seemed delighted (or it may have been amused) at my efforts and explained that in July and August his site was full of campers and it was only because it was so early in the year that there was no-one about. He said he would let us camp for free; he unlocked the ablution block and even brought us a table and two chairs, so we dined in comfort that night. During our conversation he told us he was a baker and had to be at work at five in the morning, which was why we had caught him asleep in the middle of the afternoon. We were later joined by his small son who obviously understood my French but was too shy to speak other than counting out our supper things as I set them out on the table. Although close to Porto airport, we saw only a few planes overhead, we were more disturbed by the noise of some mopeds which seemed to be using the site as a short cut.

Porto was not a pleasant experience. From our map we could see that the only practical crossing of the Rio Douro was by the city's bridge, an alternative would be another forty kilometres upstream, which would have added double that to our journey. We did not find the Porto that travel brochures describe, instead we found a bustling commercial city, full of traffic and noise. We did see evidence of the Port wine trade, the traditional boats pictured as carrying barrels moored by the river banks but they may have been more for the benefit of photographers than for their original purpose. We decided the brochure writers must be fifty years out of date, or perhaps they ignore the noise and traffic which we were not able to do. We did see some most attractive old buildings as we entered the city; most remarkable was a church entirely covered in blue tiles at the cross-roads where we started to walk. Finding our way through the city was very confusing, but we knew we had to cross the river and we thought we should go downhill to find it. The city centre was a mixture of stark modern and elegant old buildings. We found a town map which confirmed we were heading in the right direction. Expecting to go downhill to cross the bridge, we actually found ourselves on the upper level of the great double-decker iron bridge. It was after lunch in a peaceful park where we basked in the sun and wrote postcards, that the stress really began.

First we had to find the signs for Coimbra, the next major town on our route southwards; this we did but via a short stretch of motorway. As we could find no alternative, we had to go on to the next junction. After that, we found the N1, a hot, dusty and very densely-travelled road without proper hard shoulders. There followed over twenty-five kilometres of continuous suburban sprawl alongside this horrid road accompanied by nose-to-tail traffic (mostly lorries) and of course we were complaining of the heat. Not only hot, we were becoming exhausted and we realised much later in the day that, as we had only had water to drink, our blood sugar level was probably getting too low. Finally, near to San Jao, the countryside opened out and after three attempts we found somewhere to camp wild. This was the corner of a field, above a road but sheltered by Eucalyptus trees, where we settled down to a substantial supper. Over our meal we studied the map to find a different route using yellow (more minor) roads. There was unanimous agreement that the N1 should be abandoned; minor roads would probably mean more hills, rougher surfaces, less direct routing, but would definitely be more peaceful.

South to Aveiro we followed the yellow N109 which ran parallel to the coast. We had to rejoin the Nl at Aveiro to cross the Vouga estuary as the minor roads had no bridges or ferries. These coastal roads were predominantly and surprisingly flat and the vegetation very variable. Travelling south we saw more and more spring flowers, golden gorse, broom and lupins, with a sprinkling of pink clover. We were having increasing difficulty in finding food shops. Mostly when we did find them, they were hidden away up side streets, petrol stations were far more in evidence!

Our only official campsite between Vila do Conde and Evora was at Praia de Mira; as *Praia* means beach, (as in Spanish *Playa* and French *Plage*) it was by the sea about four kilometres from Mira down a very bumpy road. It would probably be very full at weekends during the season but on this Good Friday there were just enough campers to ensure the facilities were open. Warm water to shower and horror of horrors – a mirror! I had not seen my face since Santiago and during that week it had been exposed to much weather. What I saw that afternoon was enough to make any self-respecting brick blanche, but at least I was not peeling! It was at this site that we made a useful discovery: abandoned tent pegs – that would be a feature of the many hard-grounded sites, which we turned to our advantage. On the hard and often sandy ground our pegs would often bend rather than be pushed in and many were becoming unusable.

It was during our evening at Praia de Mira, when we had walked into the village to have a drink at the bar, that we first saw a cart pulled by a cow. It seemed so unusual to us. We had seen plenty of horse-drawn carts in Spain and so far in Portugal, but this was one of the poorer areas of the country. However the following day we saw an even stranger sight. We were used to seeing horses pulling ploughs, we had seen the cow pulling a cart but now we came across a human-powered plough. A large man was wearing the horse's harness pulling the plough, while his woman stumbled along behind trying to guide the furrow. As we cycled past, he snarled and appeared to growl a challenge to Peter, who averted his gaze, started to whistle and pretended not to have seen anything. Had we found *Weetabix* in Portugal he might have accepted the challenge or snarled back. It is strange to reflect that in this supposed age of great technology and wealth some Europeans are still having to use such basic methods.

Figuera de Foz; we liked the name of the town at the mouth of the Rio Mondego but we decided to take the road that bypassed the urban part. This took us along a dual-carriageway and over the enormous bridge which spanned the river before the estuary opened out. It was a great suspension bridge built to allow shipping to pass up the river from which we could see for miles (sorry, kilometres) over the flat and windswept land. Continuing south, we passed inland of a range of low hills, the Pinhai de Leira. These pine covered hills led us to a wild site in amongst the pine woods, where we first saw evidence of resin-collecting, slits in the tree trunks, below which hung little clay pots.

Easter Sunday saw us pedalling down the N1 again, heading in the direction of the country's capital. We had no intention of cycling into Lisbon but we had hoped to visit our neighbour's cousin who lives on the West side of the Tejo valley a good half day's ride from the city. If possible we would visit Lisbon, but only by public transport. I managed to contact Esme by phone, but unfortunately she was leaving for England on the day when we would be in her area, so we would be unable to meet up. That afternoon we saw our first real hills since leaving Spain, the Sierra dos Canderos; luckily we did not have to climb them as our road ran alongside.

No longer having any reason to carry on towards Lisbon, we had another 'route-re-planning session' over tea. Working on the principle that cyclists and cities do not mix, and with memories of Porto still fresh in our minds, we decided to go inland and make for Evora, a town about hundred kilometres to the east of Lisbon. This would in fact take us back to the original route which we had mapped out before the idea of visiting Esme had been presented to us. We estimated Evora to be two days' ride away – this proved correct and meant two more wild nights. The first we spent in an olive grove where we were kept awake much of the night by owls. I could distinguish at least four different calls, but the main protagonist was, I think, a youngster with an insatiable appetite, who was calling to be fed from dusk to dawn. I also felt sure he had been placed in the tree immediately above us and told on no account was he to move.

The second was in a cork-oak wood, an area of well spaced trees interspersed with flowers, yellow, pink and minty-scented purple ones. We had seen cork-oaks, one or two of them previously, but this site gave us a chance to see them close up. These trees must have been harvested before, as most of them were growing a second or even third 'coat' around their trunk. It surprised us how thick and soft the new growing cork was. That afternoon Peter had seen a discarded piece of cork with holes where the bottle corks had been punched out, now we saw where they all came from. The same afternoon we had experienced quite heavy showers from which we had had to shelter, (thank heavens for Portuguese bus shelters), but by the evening the sun had come out and we were able to dry out and enjoy one of the best Portuguese evenings.

The day we entered Evora was the day we first saw egrets. First we noticed a few birds in a field, looking like white herons, too far away to make a positive identification. A bit farther on we came up to a stand of trees from which came a sociable cackling sound that reminded me of the rookery at home only the occupants were white. As we reached the trees, we realised it was an 'egretry'. We could not tell how many birds there were but they must have been numbered in hundreds. They all seemed to be very busy caring for their nests and young and chattering away to each other. There were even a few storks as lodgers.

We found that day's other wildlife not so delightful. At every homestead were guard dogs, always ferocious-sounding and sometimes more. It was while we were riding along minding our own business that Peter spotted a rather large one running out of a group of buildings and across the field, apparently converging with our route at a most alarming rate. Luckily there was the hedge between us – or so we thought, but he knew where he was going, straight to the gap, but he was just too late. Once he reached the road he stopped running and we pedalled away as fast as we could, feeling relieved, as we did not want to experience a dog attack at close quarters.

Evora and Beja were two most attractive walled towns where we found good campsites. Riding into the first we were thankful that we could at last have a 'weekend' after nine consecutive days of cycling. We felt we must have been pretty fit by this time to be able to have done it. We were really in need of a proper site, I had suffered a puncture in the final yards of the day's journey but more than anything else, we desperately needed showers. We also wanted a few days' rest to shop and sight-see and Evora fitted the bill perfectly. I wasted no time with getting tea or such niceties. Just a few minutes after pitching the tent I was in the steaming shower – no time limit on this one and I made up for all those unwashed nights!

It was not until nearly bed time that we realised that we were camped next to a dog's holiday home! Their supper time came just after ours and the noise (of anticipation) that came over the wall was tremendous. We had no idea of just how many were in residence but it sounded like a very large number. Whether some missed out on the food or whether they were just naturally noisy, we don't know, but they kept on barking and howling well into the night!

Our rest day at Evora was a wet one but I still managed to do some laundry while Peter mended the puncture and did a few maintenance jobs. We met an English family in a luxurious camper van who invited us in for coffee. They were a retired couple and her sister, who had spent the winter on the Algarve, where the warmth alleviated her arthritis. We had heard of people selling their houses to live in a caravan but this was the first time we had met any who had actually done it. Because of her illness they only spend the summers in England and their home fitted into about fifteen feet by eight feet. They seemed very happy and carefree and they told us about sites and sights to look out for on the Algarve, which we expected to reach in a few days' time.

The afternoon was a little drier, so we spent a few hours looking round the town. I had hoped to see the cathedral but it was locked, instead we found a church dedicated to St Francis which had lovely frescoes. This church had a 'chapel of bones' adjacent to it. Apparently there are three such chapels, all completely decorated with bones excavated from nearby cemeteries. They are stuck to the walls and roof to form patterns as other Portuguese buildings are tiled. I found it quite horrible, macabre and almost evil. I was very glad to escape back into the cobbled streets of the town, vowing I would not see either of the others. During the evening we phoned Cathie and Guy, our friends who we were to meet in the Algarve later in the week. It was another expensive phone call made from the site office. We later discovered that they start the meter as one enters the booth and not when the person called answers; the first two calls we had made were unanswered.

Before we left Evora, we also met a Scottish couple resident in Australia, also in a caravanette, who were spending several months exploring Europe the easy way. They had also been to Santiago (but much more recently) and were going to Italy as well. They passed us on the road to Beja with much hooting and waving.

After our rest at Evora, it was another eighty-three kilometres ride to Beja but not a hard one. We left in the chilly damp of early morning, needing gloves, but within a couple of hours, it was shorts weather. The road from Evora was excellent for the first ten kilometres or so, until we rounded a corner and found the cobbles. We had become used to finding cobbled streets in towns but this was the first we had seen of them right out in the country. On reflection, we realised that probably all roads had been built on these 'sets' and were we not lucky there had been improvements? This consolation did nothing to ease the strain on wrists and backsides and we were so glad when the indifferent tarmac appeared again. How good, too, that it was not raining.

We found hills around Portel and it was with them that the landscape made another dramatic change. From the agricultural plains, the scenes began to look quite Mediterranean. Bare hills, red earth with little grass but rock roses and stubby trees. The temperature had also increased and again we basked in the sun before coming down again onto more plains to reach Beja in plenty of time to pitch camp before supper. Just before reaching Beja, we were approached by an energetic cyclist almost leaping along the road in his excitement at seeing us. He was a young German cycling alone from Faro on a ten day circuit hoping to go into Spain for a few days before returning for his flight home. He must have been lonely, as he had plenty to say to us, including describing his night in a hostelry where he had been served sheep's head for supper.

Beja is not as old a town as Evora; our campsite was within walls and in the centre of the town, but surprisingly quiet. On the following morning, we could not get our Visa card to communicate so we had to change a £20 note. We had found the cost of living in Portugal more expensive than we had anticipated and it was less easy to get money out of the holes-in-the-wall. We hoped it would be better for the rest of the expedition, as we did not want to eat into the reserve of traveller's cheques for day-to-day living.

The road from Beja to Ourique was probably the main one from the centre of Portugal to the south. The N391 is a well surfaced road for much of its distance, but there were sections where the familiar yellow "road works ahead" signs would appear with their awful patches of temporary surfaces, but at least there were always men working there, which gives the signs a sense of purpose. Ourique appeared to be the 'Gateway to the Algarve', a small town set on a steep hill, up which we had to struggle to find food. We reached it in the heat of the early afternoon, to find there was only one shop and that quite expensive, but at least it was open which was a relief. By this time we had realised that we must have found the sun. Most of the afternoons were becoming hot and we were beginning to think about siestas. We had been told that about twenty-five to thirty metres beyond Ourique we would find the Santa Clara lakes, which would be lovely for wild camping, but by 4.30pm we were still over ten kilometres away, so we looked around for a 'wild site' a little closer. It had become too hot and we were too tired to go several miles uphill to the lake and we were in good open country. Not far off the road, we found a track and off that, a small patch of level ground beside a stream with a ruined building against which we camped. We christened this site 'Frog Stream', as there were countless tiny croaking frogs which kept up a loud chorus all the time we were there.

We had realised that the 'Gateway to the Algarve' is one with gateposts in the form of a range of hills which we struggled to cross on our way to Quarteira and the coast. We had chosen the IP2 road as the most direct and hopefully the least steep crossing but nevertheless it was steep for our heavily-laden bikes. The hills had become very Mediterranean in appearance, especially once we had started to descend. What a lovely smooth descent it was, such a good road that we clocked up thirty-five kilometres before our elevenses. Our break that morning was in the comfort of a rest area (with table and benches) where we watched a diminutive lady trucker setting up and driving off an enormous rig.

With the picturesque hills behind us, it was onto the 'Algarve Main Road' to battle our way eastwards against a headwind which, though welcome for its coolness, was otherwise exhausting. So glad we were that we had heard of a campsite at Quateira which we reached before a late lunch, as I had not the energy to go further that day. It was a real resort town, large modern hotel and apartment blocks with the campsite hidden away at the far end of town. In all we had ridden seventy-two kilometres before lunch, but who wants to set records anyway?

The city of Faro, and thank goodness we cycled through it on a Sunday morning, the headwinds of the previous day had eased off a bit and the road was very gentle so we made good progress. The signing around Faro was far better than we had come to expect and we only went round in a circle once before finding the right road. This was the day when we met up with Cathie and Guy, the friends from our home village. They were out on a week's holiday which coincided very neatly with our progress. They had given us the address but had not had any directions to give us, so we were a bit anxious as to how we would find them. Taveira was the town on the address, so we stopped for lunch just short of there. Whilst relaxing on the grass, we witnessed a near accident; a cyclist almost knocked off his bike by a motorist making a turn far too fast.

Once in Taveira we showed the address to a pedestrian who directed us on five kilometres to a newly-completed holiday village where we found the apartment block very easily. It was not so easy to find our friends, they were out and as they were not expecting to see us until the following day, had left no message. Leaving them a note to say we would be back the next day, we set off to find the campsite shown on the map, only to find it was no longer there. In desperation, we returned to Cabanas to find Cathie and Guy returning from the day on the beach with their family.

The welcome they gave us can only be described as tremendous; they really took us under their wing. For nearly twenty-four hours we were able to relax and become holidaymakers, pampered ones, and it was wonderful. They brought us in, sat us down and produced tea and we caught up on all the village gossip. They had phoned my parents just before leaving, so were able to reassure us that they were well and promised to tell them of our progress on their return. Their apartment had a swimming pool in which we all played for an hour before Cathie produced a stretched meal of cyclist's proportions. It was only when we were attired in our swimming things that we realised how much weight we had lost. We had not really seen our bodies recently and now we could see ribs on each other we had never seen before! They fed us, they took us to the pub for an impromptu karaoke session and to round off the evening, gave us a space on the floor to lay our airbed and even a bit of foam mattress to pad it when the inevitable early morning deflation happened. Finally, before we left in the morning, they gave us a substantial breakfast and sent us on our way rejoicing. It was an evening to remember, eating chicken on the rooftop terrace, watching the sun go down and drinking local wine from the most enormous bottle. All the while daughter Sam was recording it on camera; a series of pictures was on display long before we ever saw them.

The following morning we had only a couple of hours until we reached the border again. We may not have taken the best route through Portugal, as we had not found the countryside as interesting as we had hoped. True we had avoided Lisbon which would probably have proved an interesting city had we not been on a cycling tour. Our main goal had been to make progress before the summer heat took over. We regretted that we had not seen the pilgrim town of Fatima but we only heard of it after we had passed the area; another case of not doing the research thoroughly enough. We had, however, travelled the whole length of the country and experienced a variety of weathers. We had needed gloves on many early mornings; we had been hot but we had been really exhausted on only one day. Sometimes the weather had been indifferent but never unpleasant. We had spent six nights on sites, six camping wild and one in civilisation. Thus our wild nights had subsidised the costed ones. Our cost of living had averaged £7 each per day, with no extras except the two phone calls.

However, we had found some gentle countryside, some windy plains and some lovely scented orange groves especially in the last two days. It had been fairly difficult to buy food, especially in the north, and surprisingly expensive for some items, mainly cheese which was for us a staple. Roads had been on the whole poor, at times atrocious, though that did not seem to make any difference to the motorists, who drove flat out from A to B whatever the conditions. We found the language quite different from Spanish and more difficult to understand, but my slight knowledge of French helped. On the whole, people were friendly, helpful and relaxed. We decided that Portugal was a country to pass through rather than re-visit.

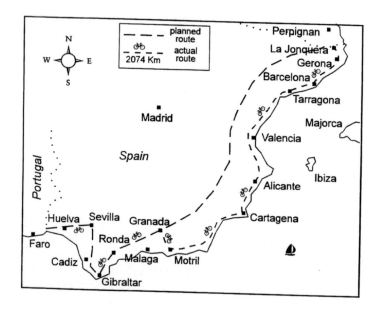

Chapter 5 Spain again…and more rain

We had been in Portugal for two weeks all but a day. We had not felt really comfortable with the Algarve, as we felt our rather scruffy appearance did not suit the smart holiday villages and there had not been enough campsites, so we left the country on the morning after we had seen our friends – a very different border crossing this time, by ferry boat. It was an easy ride into Vila Real de Santo Antonio (we even saw a campsite) near to where we passed a black and white striped lighthouse on the way to the ferry. A small wooden ferry boat took us across the Rio Guardiana from Vila Real to Ayamonte. It could have carried two small cars but there were only two-wheeled vehicles this trip – our bikes. About half an hour of chugging across the water and we could see the road crossing which was…a motorway, but we felt much more relaxed. So far our borders had been crossed by a large ferry (Plymouth to Santander), a bridge and now a tiny ferry, we wondered what else was in store.

Pushing our bikes back into Spain, we found the change office where they took all our Portuguese money, even the coins, which surprised and pleased us. Ayamonte started off with cobbles, but as soon as we saw the signs for Huelva, the tarmac started again and we were off into a landscape of orange orchards and strawberry fields. It was the scent of strawberries that told us it was time for lunch which had to be taken in a small and very scruffy lay-by close to a large orange orchard. There we watched enormous refrigerated lorries driving into the fields to load up the crates of fruit for despatch to far away places. Over the next few weeks, we were to be surrounded by oranges as we cycled up the south and east coasts of Spain but I never tired of their smell or taste. It was at this stage of the journey that Peter began to suspect he was married to a Fruit Freak. As we progressed, I found a great variety of delicious fruits indigenous to the different stages of the journey. We had already found kiwis at Santiago, pears in Portugal and oranges throughout. I had to be careful to remember that there was a limit to the amount my panniers would hold. I just love fruit and the fresher the better, but more of that later.

After our lunch we carried on for only another fifteen kilometres before seeing a campsite. It was easy to recognise because there were three tents erected near to the gate. In we cycled and booked for a couple of nights as we felt it was time for another 'weekend'. After a refreshing beer, the owner said we could pitch anywhere. It was only much later that we realised we were the only campers, as the tents we had seen were decoys. We thought it most amusing and we were to see many more as we travelled on. The emptiness of the site was an advantage as we were given sole use of a private bathroom, intended for use by disabled campers. It had the ultimate luxury, a hot shower.

After tea we set off with empty panniers, a strange sensation, as it was the first time we had left camp to 'go shopping' like this. After six kilometres, we found Las Antillos, a brand new holiday town of freshly-painted apartment blocks, well stocked and irrigated flower beds and a golf course, but not a soul to be seen. A ghost town, a town waiting to wake up. After an exploratory circuit of the town we found one shop, (one person) and saw one or two men in a bar. It seemed so strange and empty but the season had not yet started, it would probably be full of Sevillians within a few weeks.

We had a peaceful rest day at the site and we spent much of the time walking on the beach which was separated from the campsite by a very narrow strip of woodland. Though spending the day in idleness for a change, we did take a trip into Las Antillos to make an important purchase. I was buying postcards when Peter noticed that the shop sold airbeds, and good quality individual ones of rubberised cotton, so he bought a couple to replace our troublesome vinyl double one which had been the cause of so much backache and early wake-ups. We had thought of acquiring a piece of foam rubber to place under our backs where we always hit the ground, but when he saw these airbeds, he made an instant and wise decision. As we had now moved into warmer climes and only needed one sleeping bag to use as a quilt, the other could be used as protection from the stones beneath the beds, and our days of awakening with that sinking feeling were over!

It had been a strange couple of nights – on a deserted site near a deserted town. It was the first of the southern Spanish campsites, a factor which was reflected in the cost, 2480 pesetas for two nights – £15.50. Never mind, we made up for it by spending the following four nights camping wild, although we had expected to find more official sites at this stage.

From Las Antillos, we had to navigate towards Seville but avoiding the Isla Mayor, the large marshy area between the mouths of the Rios Tinto and Guadalquivir. Much of it is national park, crossed by numerous smaller rivers but no roads. Thus we had quite a lengthy detour as we wished to rejoin the coastal road near Cadiz to head down to Gibraltar. Unfortunately, our map showed us no easy route around Seville. We had to go well north to get round Huelva and to avoid another complicated estuary system of the Rios Odiel and Tinto which flow into the Atlantic near the town. From here, there is a motorway direct from Huelva to Sevilla which has an N road alongside, which we had to find and follow. This road, the N431, although it looked quite direct and uninteresting on the map, proved to be a good one and gave us an excellent wild site quite unexpectedly.

We had really been clocking up the distances, over ninety a day at this stage, so we knew we had become very fit. Just after the estuaries we approached the Rio Tinto (after which our favourite wines are named – Vino Tinto) and the reason for its name was all too clear. I had never seen red water before. Taking its colour from the sandstone over which it flowed, this was even redder than the sandstone of our native Devon. We crossed the river near the town of Nuebla, an old red-walled city. It was such a shame we did not take time off to explore the city. We later discovered we could have spent an hour or two looking around and taking photos as we had to waste that time at Paterna de Contado waiting for their long siesta to finish and for the shops to open. The trouble was that we were always so keen to press on and put as much distance under our wheels as possible; that afternoon was one when we regretted our haste.

During our enforced rest, we sat in the palm-shaded square looking at an exquisite blue and white tiled church before provisioning and going off to find a resting place for the night. It was becoming quite difficult to find wild sites, nearly as difficult as trying to find official ones in this part of Spain, as we were just out of the main holiday areas. After about five kilometres, we came across the only wood in this part of the country and in its centre was a wide ditch which was just the right size for our camp. In the bank of the ditch was a warren of rabbit holes which was visited by a hunter/trapper whilst we cooked our supper. He engaged Peter in conversation whilst looking to see if he'd caught anything, I was afraid he might wish to join our meal but he departed before it was ready. We saw no more of him that evening but we were a little nervous, so we surrounded our tent with sticks which would snap if anyone approached. What did disturb us during the night was another form of life – foxes barking and coughing through the depths of the darkness. Then towards morning it was the rabbits, who decided it was safe to come out and nibble the vegetation very close to the tent and made strange little scuffling noises alongside my pillow.

I have not mentioned before the dead animals left by the roadside but I suppose the heat made them more noticeable. We must have passed numerous sad corpses of all sizes, and our sensitive English noses and my squeamishness found it most upsetting. Some had obviously been there a long time, desiccated and often flattened, and no one had bothered to remove them as would have been the case in England.

The road to Sanlucar la Mayor showed a section with four red Xs which according to map key denoted a road with an impassable (or impossible) surface and we expected to have to look for an alternative. We were almost in the town before we realised we had passed it – yet another inaccuracy in our map. We had been resolving to buy better, larger scale maps when we could find them, so we really should have had one for that day!

Thursday, 22nd April was a memorable day. It was the day when we negotiated the Seville ring road, unintentionally. After Sanlucar we still had to follow signs for Sevilla, hoping to find the little white road which should take us to the south of the city and onto the NIV towards Gibraltar. We had no success in finding the white road and as the morning progressed we found that Sevilla was getting uncomfortably close.

Suddenly we realised that we had joined a dual carriageway which became the beginning of the ring road and we could not escape. The only way was to go with the flow, and that meant with the traffic. The dual-carriageway became six and then eight lanes and all of them with cars and lorries speeding along, carrying us with them. I was terrified, I was cycling along just in front of Peter as he kept shouting directions to me; "Follow the white line", "Keep going" and "Move over NOW". How I wished I could have shut my eyes! The worst part was where the road went up and over an enormous bridge where there was no hard shoulder. We could not get off to push, so only the adrenaline got us over that one. It probably only lasted for just over half an hour but it seemed like half a day at the time. Once we found the signs to Cadiz and moved onto the NIV, I felt like a quivering wreck, we were not able to find a place to pull off for lunch until two o'clock when the countryside appeared. What an experience! None of the towns we had been through had filled me with such fear. The shame of it was we had seen so little of Seville, just a brief glimpse of a 'Big Wheel' in the distance which must have been erected for the trade fair the previous year.

Our friends in Portugal had spoken of going to visit the trade fair site but we had seen all of Seville that we were likely to. We had been advised to avoid the city because of crime against foreign tourists: in fact we were warned of the same in Barcelona but did not feel at all threatened. Once clear of Seville, we followed the NIV for the remainder of the day, another forty kilometres and after another wild camp between some bushes rather too close to the road, struck out across country towards Gibraltar.

It was nearly four days from Seville to Gibraltar, crossing some of the windiest country we had yet encountered. It was mainly a countryside of low hills, though some were not as low as others. By avoiding Cadiz, we were able to follow the C343 for a day and a half. To begin with we could see Mount Pinar, 1600 metres high, in the distance and we hoped it would stay distant, though it added interest to the horizon. The C343 proved to be quite a rough surfaced road but a quiet and most interesting one. The first village we saw perched on a small hill had the first of the pictorial signs we were to see so often in this part of Spain. It was a day of 'over the hills and far way', the largest town of the day being Arcos de la Frontera. We had the best view of this town once we had passed it and looked back to see the walled town perched picturesquely on its own hill looking like a medieval fortress. According to the map, Arcos has a 'parador' (a rather posh hotel) but we ignored this fact and carried on for another thirty-five kilometres before finding our own little oasis surrounded by cacti.

The day had become tougher as we had continued; not only had the hills become steeper after lunch, but a wind had risen, blowing as a headwind, and was competing with the awful roads to slow us down. We had one stretch of road that had disappeared beneath the sand and was so rutted that we were almost down to walking pace, so by 4.15pm we were more than ready to call a halt. We found that the only place on this road that was not fenced was amongst a small patch of cacti, between some fields, and judging by the noises in the night, it was close to a farm. Although hot when we arrived, it was not long before we were sheltering from our first rain since leaving Portugal. Was this an omen? After a day of rough-going, we felt really pleased with our bicycles, they were going so well. We had travelled nearly 2000 kilometres in almost a calendar month. The problems resulting from the accident in Lugo seemed to have been overcome. Peter's wheel building had really succeeded, and I was used to the slight kink in the pedal shank. There were as yet no recurrences of the bottom bracket clicks and our tyres were not yet worn enough to give us the frequent punctures we were to suffer very soon.

The C343 led us south as far as Vejer de la Frontera, where it met the N340 from Cadiz to Algeciras, another red road where we found a shop selling Camping Gaz (so pleased we were that we bought four canisters). The best sight near Verjer was a real cowboy on a horse. We had seen several pictures of mounted cowboys on the signboards we had passed, but it was something else to see one in the flesh rounding up some cattle. The bad points of the day were that Peter had two punctures before lunch and that it rained. In fact it rained too much for us to boil up for our mid-morning cuppa and it had turned quite cold, so we had to curtail our lunch stop and get moving again quickly. During the afternoon, the wind got up again as a strong sidewind. This made the going very hard and at times I felt it was rather dangerous as it seemed to blow us off course, and even threatened to blow me over. As a result I hit a 'low' about 4pm and Peter decided we would camp by the road just in the lee of a high bank. The clouds were heavy and threatening and the mountains were shrouded in clouds, but in the gaps between, we could see some large birds wheeling overhead. They looked like eagles but I later saw reference to honey buzzards, so I decided that was probably what they were.

We had only just pitched the tent when the storm hit us, the heavy looking clouds emptied on us and the winds grew to the strongest yet. We had not had time to empty the panniers, so all our belongings were out in the rain. We were sitting in the tent, holding on to it for all we were worth, praying that it would hold together, watching the curved hoops supporting the nylon curving all ways and wincing as the thunder and lightning fought a battle in the hills around us. The whole storm lasted nearly three and a half hours but the tent thankfully survived and it did not tear, which was our greatest fear, nor did it leak. The contents of the panniers (which had leaked) came out in differing degrees of sogginess. The main casualty was Peter's passport which will bear evidence of that evening until it expires. The maps (as yet unused) were also very wet, but our sleeping bags thankfully remained fairly dry on the insides. This had been the worst day for weather so far; at least on the day when it had snowed, it had improved later, on this day there was not enough time for improvement before dark. Our belated and substantial supper improved our spirits no end. On the occasions when I was finding things too much, and there were a few days when, for a short while at least, I would have liked to go home, I found that rest and/or food restored me.

Sunday 25th April started with another thunderstorm but by nine o'clock it had passed and we could get under way. We discovered we had been quite close to a town called Facina though we doubted if it would have offered anywhere to camp. Before mid-morning we had passed many, many campsites around Tarifa, the windsurfing capital of Spain, but we had not known that we had been only about six or seven kilometres from the first of them! We had been three nights without a shower and were feeling rather smelly, though we had managed to catch some rainwater in our cooking pots to wash faces and hands. it had been too cold to expose any more than that.

Once the storm cleared and the sun came out, we began to feel a great deal more optimistic about the prospect of being able to reach Gibraltar that day, even though the map showed two mountain passes to be crossed. At Tarifa we had our first glimpse of the Straits and the North African coast. There was a ferry service from Tarifa to Tangier but we were not tempted, we were on our way to Gibraltar. There were still the mountains to cross and, by the look of the clouds, still some rain to be endured. We were chased by a shower as we climbed up to the first pass, the Passo del Cubrito at 340 metres; it did catch us but was not too drenching. Climbing up this side of the mountains, we were most interested to see the wind turbines. All along the ridges and hill tops like a forest of trees with whirling branches; there they were utilising the windiest area of Spain. They were particularly pleasing to us as we are in favour of renewable energy and feel our authorities should take a leaf out of the Spanish energy book. We could see a cluster in the distance, close to Facina, which presumably powered that town. Those all about us must have been connected to power lines carrying the electricity to other areas. Those we passed closest to did not seem very noisy, which I believe is one of the main objections to proposals to erect them in our own country.

After climbing off my soapbox and back onto my bicycle again, we had a short descent before climbing the second pass, Passo del Bujeo (320 metres) after a second shower. We spent most of this second shower under a bus shelter which we shared with an old man who was smoking a powerful brand of cigarette whilst we brewed up our elevenses. After the Passo del Bujeo, there came the wonderful downhill run to Algeciras. Just as we started, we had our first glimpse of The Rock as it rises 430 metres out of the sea. What excitement! We had both seen it only as a photographed subject and it is such a feeling to see something so famous in real life. We were surprised and pleased at the speedy run down to Algeciras, an excellent road down to the bay, where we could see a large number of ships at anchor. We took the road which bypassed the town and actually passed a campsite but it was only noon; we were going to Gibraltar and nothing was going to stop us.

Chapter 6 The Rock

We thought the Bay of Algeciras really most impressive as we swept around it on the Autovia. There were ships of various sizes anchored in the large natural harbour. Having studied the map, we had hoped to find a campsite at either the romantic sounding San Roque or La Ligne de Conception. Instead we found San Roque to be an industrial town surrounding a smelly oil refinery with smoking stacks and flaring towers and La Ligne we saw as a rather scruffy border town. We cycled the length of the latter being sure there must be a site but even at the far end all we could find was a bottle-strewn beach where we sat in the cold wind to eat a hurried lunch. For company we had a few scruffy seagulls searching the rubbish and some armed soldiers patrolling the beach on the look out for some miscreant or other; we were glad we did not come into that category.

The wind was too strong for us to relish the prospect of returning to the site at Algeciras, so we decided to treat ourselves to a couple of days holiday on Gibraltar, even if it meant splashing out on the cost of an hotel. There was some justification, as the following day would be our seventh wedding anniversary and the day after, my birthday. It was quite exciting crossing over the causeway to Gibraltar, postcards and the mention of 'Gib' had been frequent in my early childhood, as my father visited it often when flying in the Royal Air Force but now here we were, actually cycling onto 'The Rock'. So many signs in English made us feel really at home. Being the northerly pillar of Hercules gives an air of romance to this limestone mountain as it rises so steeply from the sea.

As we cycled towards the customs post on this windy and rainy Sunday afternoon, our first concern was to find an hotel, so Peter asked the border policeman who directed us to the Bristol Hotel in Cathedral Square. As luck would have it, the proprietor himself was a cyclist, so when Peter mentioned the 'problem' of having little luggage but two bicycles, he was more than happy to accommodate them in his storeroom. There was even a lift to take our panniers upstairs and within a very few minutes, I had fallen into a hot shower and was relishing the prospect of being able to get things dry. In fact I spent so long luxuriating in the shower that Peter came in to ask if I had dissolved myself yet.

Civilisation for a couple of nights; real beds with room to walk around them – upright! By the time I had vacated the shower, Peter had discovered Sky television with the news in English and was catching up on John Major's latest exploits; England seemed so remote though we had only been away just over a month. We were to find Gibraltar to be just like an English town set down at the edge of the Mediterranean. The streets were so narrow you could not tell which side the cars were driving and the shops had so many familiar names, *Marks & Spencer* and *Safeway* among the most prominent. After hanging up some of the wettest of our equipment, putting on our remaining dry clothes and having a very leisurely tea, we ventured forth to start exploring the town. It seemed to consist of one main street with several smaller ones going off at right angles. Very close to the hotel, we saw a sign outside the Methodist church informing us that there was to be an evening service at seven o'clock, so we resolved to be there. Although, being a Sunday afternoon, the English shops were not open, we did find a Spanish one selling *Brook Bond Tea* and *Kellogg's Corn Flakes*; what a feast we were in for at breakfast. It was interesting to find things priced in two currencies simultaneously.

The evening service at the Methodist Church was very much like some of our less formal ones at home and we felt very comfortable joining in. It was so good to be a participant in a church service rather than just a sightseer, as we had been recently in the churches we had visited in Spain and Portugal. They made us so welcome and we found it almost overwhelming to hear so much English spoken after having heard only our own voices for so long. We rounded off the evening with a meal of scampi and chicken in a Chinese restaurant. It was to have been fish and chips, but they had run out during the afternoon.

During that night, I can recall that I had my first food dream, the first of many. I must have reached just about my lowest weight and I was to wake up on many occasions having dreamt of what I would eat the following day. Maybe it was the knowledge that we were going to have a proper breakfast with cereal and milk instead of just bread and jam. It was strange to wake with a ceiling overhead and to be in real beds for the first time for over a month. We had asked the hotel reception about the nearest launderette, but after we had walked for the necessary fifteen minutes we found it was no longer operating.

We carried everything back again and I set up my own in the bathroom basin – with hot running water it was easy. Before long we had used all the clothes hangers and had festoons of clothes drying off whilst the sleeping bags were still draped over the shower cubicle. I think we were a bit disappointed that it was still so cold, but it was explained to us that Gibraltar is always windy due to the air funnelling in and out of the Straits.

After lunch the rain cleared and we spent the afternoon doing touristy things. We were very keen to go up in the cable car to the summit. Although I suffer from vertigo, I felt fine in the enclosed lift, unlike one of our fellow passengers. There were amazing views as we sailed up the cliff face, the ships in the harbour retreating until they were minute specks and the cars on the streets below becoming more and more like toys. At the top is the nature reserve, from where we could see across to the mountains over which we had climbed twenty-four hours before – they were still being rained on!

Having come up the easy way, we took the long footpath down again. There were many viewing points, so we could see not only back towards Spain, but over the harbours, the airport and the town as well as the North African coast. Our first stop on the way down was St Michael's Cave, vast limestone caverns with rock formations in weird and wonderful shapes. The stalactites and stalagmites are tastefully lit by changing coloured lights while dramatic classical music is played. Indeed one part of the cavern is set out as a concert hall with rows of seats facing a 'stage' from which musical performances are given. It would have been lovely to attend one but none were programmed for that day – we had to content ourselves with listening to the canned music being played at the time which was very effective. In another part of the cave is a waxwork display of a Neolithic family at home, and in another, a cut and polished section of stalagmite can be examined. The architecture almost rivalled some of the cathedrals and churches we had seen. This was just part of the thirty-three miles of tunnels within the Rock, much of them not open to view.

Continuing our descent, the path took us through the apes' den where we stopped to talk to the residents. Everywhere were signs warning "Do Not Feed", many near to the packets of ape food for sale. Some of the animals were very shy, but one came right up and started talking to me, Peter has a photo of us in earnest conversation.

They are a great deal smaller than I had imagined, I understand they are not strictly apes but a form of monkey. Further down we passed a large gun still in its emplacement, dating from the beginning of the century but disarmed in 1954. There were still many MOD Property signs around the path as it completed its descent and brought us out very close to Cathedral Square.

The youth of Gibraltar seem to spend their time driving their cars up and down the main street with radios blaring so loudly that the ground seems to vibrate. The same car can be seen (and heard) up and down the same stretch of street constantly, as we discovered when we just sat to watch the world go by. After that whenever we heard a radio-announced car approach, one or other of us would call out "Gibraltar Car".

We finished the day with a slap-up meal at Bunter's Bar to celebrate our anniversary. It was an excellent meal though we did over-indulge a bit. There was also a noisy thunderstorm that night resulting in a power cut, but we were snug indoors this time and it did not worry us.

We had found it a bit expensive staying in the hotel, so on the morning of my birthday we packed up our panniers and made a final trip to the English supermarket. We bought some delicious rolls at the bakery department, some apples as a change from oranges and a dried emergency meal which we needed before we left Spain. I had to pass by a decorated birthday cake as being unportable; we would have to make up for it on Peter's birthday in July, wherever that would find us. We said our good-byes to the proprietor, received some advice concerning the road to Ronda and retrieved our bicycles from the storeroom where they had stayed warm and dry for the two days.

There was undoubtedly a great deal more we could have seen and done had we stayed longer but we had become so used to moving on and what with the expense of the hotel, we could not afford to stay more than the two nights. For us it was just a taste of Gibraltar, but it is nice to leave somewhere like that hoping that one day we will be able to come back and see more.

Chapter 7   Spanish Mountains and Granada

Gibraltar had marked another geographical stage on our journey, firstly because it is such a landmark on the map, and secondly, because after leaving it we met a dramatic change in the type of countryside. We had only one problem leaving the Rock, I mistook one of the navigator's instructions and turned left instead of straight on, cutting across the front of him and knocking him off, but only gently. We retraced some of the Algeciras bypass until the turning for Ronda where we headed north, along the C333. As it was my birthday, it seemed appropriate to be riding along some very English-looking roads. The C333 was the minor road up towards the mountains, the Serania de Ronda. It was the road marked on the map with a green line, denoting a picturesque route and was a scenic and gentle climb towards the still distant hills. Travelling up this road, we thought it remarkably green for southern Spain, hedged on both sides; the most notable difference between this and 'home' was the stork's nest we stopped to photograph. It was perched on top of a pylon and we could even see the youngsters peering out questioningly at us, as if wondering how we had got down there. At this time we decided that our elevenses would be more beneficial and less time-consuming if we were to drink fruit juice instead of brewing a cup of tea. It proved a sensible decision as our energy for the second part of the morning was greatly increased and we wondered why we had not thought of it before.

As we approached Jimena, where we intended to stop for lunch, we came across some road works. This time it was resurfacing by spraying tar on the road (and on us as we passed). The road had been very rough and was much in need of repair but our black specks were to be with us for a very long time. Just as the road started to become noticeably steeper, we found a perfect lunch spot overlooking Jimena a little below us. We had planned to stop near there for the night but our progress that day had been so good that we decided to carry on and find a wild site, if we could find a space level enough for the tent.

It was a pleasantly warm sunny afternoon with the hills becoming progressively steeper, and we found that we were doing more walking than pedalling. It was such a beautiful landscape we were in that there were no complaints. We saw very little traffic and by four o'clock we decided to look for a wild site. There was a little level ground under a tree all amongst wild flowers, a real botanist's paradise. Not being scientifically-minded, we just appreciated their form and colour. Close by was a well that provided us with a cold face-splash. Not far away we saw a large herd of goats, many with bells round their necks, being called in to the farm buildings for the night.

Unfortunately, our beautiful evening turned into a wet and most unpleasant night, followed by probably the most unpleasant day of the whole journey. Such a contrast to our day up towards the mountains, our day in them was horrid. It had started raining during the night and by breakfast (almost the last of our food), it looked set in for the day. We had no choice but to don our wet suits and get moving. Striking a wet tent is not so easy, nor is packing it into the confined space of the pannier. It is also much heavier to carry, but at least we did not have the weight of food to start with that morning. Our advisor at the hotel had assured us that we should see superb views, as had a friend in England from whom we had first heard of Ronda. They were both wrong as they had not anticipated the weather conditions on this particular day. We were quite lucky to find Guacin, the only village, as the rainy mist was very thick, but find it we did and its one and only food shop provided supplies to keep us going. At least with food and drink in our panniers we only had two more obstacles to overcome: the mountains and the weather.

The latter we could only describe as a proper Dartmoor 'mizzle', visibility of fifty to one hundred metres with a heavy penetrating drizzle. On we pressed, sometimes walking and sometimes riding on what seemed to be one continuous climb hour after hour. Then out of the mist appeared a brown sign with white lettering, "Passo 800 metres", our spirits lifted with this information, thinking we were now over the worst. Even the weather cheered up and we could now see a little more of the countryside around us. Sparse vegetation and barren grey rocks with many large outcrops surrounded us. We were now above the mist and could see the low clouds down to our right moving lazily along, seeming to gobble up everything both large and small in their path.

The road ahead was now visible and we could see there was still more climbing to do. After what seemed ages but was only a half an hour or so, there was another of those signs but this time it was "Passo 1000 metres" which we realised after rapid calculation meant we were 3250 feet above yesterday's sea level, almost the height of Snowdon! Surely this had to be the top – please! The countryside then opened out and we were on a small green plateau with a ruined farm over to our left, just off the road. We thought this an ideal spot for lunch as we needed some shelter from the wind, which was getting colder by the minute. Leaning the bikes against the wall we cleared a place to sit and proceeded to eat our bread and cheese. That was when it started to rain, which, added to the cold wind, made us feel very uncomfortable indeed. We both started to shiver uncontrollably and an instant decision had to be made – pack lunch away and get moving. The rain became heavier as we regained the road and remounted. That was when Peter realised that his back tyre was as flat as a pancake. He attempted to pump up the tyre, only to find his fingers were so cold he could not undo the valve cap. The situation was getting serious, we were becoming colder by the second and concerned about the possibility of exposure. It would take at least five or ten minutes to mend the puncture, that was when Peter shouted "Walk, come on, let's push, to heck with the tyre, it's expendable – we must keep warm". Not knowing how far it was to Ronda, we pushed on.

I think that was the low point of the day. Neither of us felt like talking so we pushed on in miserable sodden silence. I think I was sobbing to myself when the tune of "Onward, Christian Soldiers" started to come from my lips. It is a marvellous tempo for marching and soon I was singing and marching along, no longer miserable and I was getting warm. After about six or seven kilometres we had descended enough to be warmer and with now-thawed fingers, we were able to change Peter's tube. From thereon the day improved and the worst was over. Although the rain was still falling, we were no longer heading straight into it, the wind had eased a little and we were well past the highest point.

Within six kilometres we saw the blessed tent sign, a campsite, and there was no consulting each other. As I was in the lead, I rode straight in. Without asking what I wanted to do, Peter booked us into a bungalow for the night and it was wonderful. In fact it was like a rather large comfortable garden shed with two bedrooms, a kitchen, bathroom and luxury of all luxuries a heater! Within record time the bungalow was strewn with all our kit doing its best to get dry; fortunately we had packed most of it in plastic bags but that did not prevent damp edges on everything. At least we had a change of almost dry clothes and the towels were in not too bad a state. A hot shower and clean socks made a great deal of difference to our states of mind; we were so thankful to have found El Sur (the site) as the prospect of having to camp wild in these conditions had filled us both with dread. Who knows what the outcome might have been? Sometimes we just have to remember we are not in our twenties any more, and that night we really felt our ages. We congratulated ourselves on having survived the day and having traversed two such high passes, obviously the ones before Gibraltar had just been for practice.

Our trip into Ronda later in the evening (when it had actually stopped raining) was for essential shopping and not for the sight-seeing which we had hoped to do when we had planned to come to Ronda. For our evening meal we treated ourselves to a hot, spicy octopus stew, cooked on an almost full-sized cooker and washed down with plentiful vino tinto. Our super-fitness enabled us to shrug off the rigours of the horrendous day once we had a good meal inside us. By that stage, we were amazed at how quickly we were able to recover once we found rest and improved conditions.

The most comfortable night of the whole expedition was that one spent in the comfortable bed at the bungalow where we awoke to the sound of lighter rain on the roof. We just lay listening to it and enjoying the comfort. Would we be able to move on or would we have to stay another day? At eight o'clock that morning we did not really care. As we sat and had tea in bed, from a real tea pot, we drew the curtains and took our first look out of the window at the scenery. Yes, we could see the mountains and they were lovely. Feeling greatly revived, we awarded ourselves a hearty breakfast which we ate sitting at the table. Thus we felt much better about venturing forth.

We were still on the C341, which led us all over the town to get out of Ronda. There were still threatening clouds around us, so we did not feel like delaying our start. Once on the road to Campillos, we found it had very patchy surfaces and before long it was my turn for the daily puncture, only a tiny thorn, but the effect was the same, a flat back tyre. By the time we had changed the tube the weather had improved, a wonderful contrast to the previous day. Perfect cycling weather with just a few showers. The main one came whilst we were having lunch at a most convenient bus shelter, miles from anywhere but there when we most needed it. While we were munching, we saw another cycling couple coming up from the Campillos direction so we all waved – we were rather glad we had the downhill stretch ahead of us.

After we passed Teba, the countryside became full of wild flowers, pink snapdragons and scented golden broom – a real joy to the eye and so refreshing after the previous day. We felt so lucky that if ever we had a bad day it was usually followed by a really good one. As we approached Campillos, the land seemed to flatten out and intensive farming took over, much of it in sheds which, judging by the smell was undoubtedly battery hens. We could also see very few trees, so where were we going to camp for the night? After Campillos, where we drew cash (and spent a little on our next provisions) we rejoined the N342 which we had left after Arcos de la Frontera just over a week before. Then we had been facing west, now we were riding in an easterly direction. Five kilometres after Campillos we found our oasis, an olive grove a little off the road. Olives are excellent trees amongst which to site our matching tent, but to make sure of invisibility we pulled some of the recently pruned branches around us making our own mini-grove. As we suppered that night, we were a bit annoyed to realise the woman at the Ronda site had not returned our Camping Carnet, the card which proved our identity and sometimes gave us discount on site fees. We should just have to manage without it but we knew this would mean parting with our passports in future.

As we left our olive grove the next morning we saw the same car pulling into the farm drive that we had seen leaving on our arrival. We wondered if they recognised us and if so would they wonder why we had not made any progress during the last fifteen hours! As we rode on towards Antequera, a most photogenic mist was rising off the fields but our camera was not sophisticated enough to take advantage of it. All the signs were trying to entice us to go south to Malaga but not us, our sights were set on Granada, even though it was further up in the mountains. The road was winding around some hills and up over others. Every time we came to a descent, we hoped it would not take us too far down, as that would only increase the next climb.

The longest and steepest of these hills was to cause a major problem that day. The warning sign at the top stated that the descent was for five kilometres and that it was a steep one. That meant brakes. About half way down I heard a terrific explosion behind me and, not knowing what I would find, I turned round to see Peter thankfully still upright and examining his wheel which had exploded. We had heard of exploding rims but the first experience of it is very alarming. The action of brake on rim causes a build up of heat thus expanding the air within the tyre...and bang. Being heavily loaded, when the wheel hit the road the rim was forced outwards causing distortion so we had even more of a problem. Both inner and outer tyres were wrecked, the inner almost completely shredded, so we put on new ones and limped the rest of the way down the hill to a large restaurant, arriving at the same time as the next rain.

Glad to have a drink and shelter for our lunch, we reassessed the day. We chatted to members of an English coach party who were on their way back to the coast from Granada. Had they been going in the opposite direction we would have asked for a lift. The next town was Loja, but on questioning the staff at the restaurant, we discovered that there were no campsites there. Next, Peter asked about rates at hostels and on hearing they were similar to our Ronda bungalow, we thought that would be the answer. So off again in the rain for the short distance to Loja where we found a hostel which provided all we needed for the night. The hostel was another new experience. We had frequently seen hostels but always bypassed them in favour of campsites. This time we felt in need of rather more shelter than our tent could afford, especially as we had some comprehensive repairs to make to Peter's wheel. The first thing we were shown was a large underground garage which was unlocked for our bikes. It was almost empty, so there was a vast space for us to remove the damaged wheel and take it with the tool bag upstairs to our room. The room, though fairly basic, was actually a little larger than the hotel room we had stayed in. To my surprise, it had its own bathroom and a tiny veranda which overlooked the mountains, a lovely view when the rain cleared. Peter set to work with pliers and spoke key to straighten the distorted rim which was quite a long job and finished it off with the file to smooth out the remaining crinkles in the rim's surface. A perfectly smooth finish could not be achieved, though this later proved to be a slight advantage, as the brakes functioned better on the rougher rim.

Once again Peter had made a repair which was to last beyond the duration of the trip.

Later in the evening the rain eased off somewhat, so we went in search of a supermarket (or supper shop); the big advantage of having all the camping equipment with us was that we were able to buy our usual tinned food and cook wherever we were. The only place we did not use our cooker was on the ferry boat over to Greece. We also found a bicycle shop to enquire about a replacement wheel in case the repair was not satisfactory once the wheel was back on the bike. It turned out that it would be impossible to get the exact size, the nearest would be a 700C which is close but not really good enough, so we prayed the repair would suffice. Many of the streets in Loja were stepped, others were very narrow and twisty; it would have been a town to fascinate us under better circumstances. As it was, we just wanted to buy food and get back into the dry to consume it.

The following day we cycled the remaining sixty kilometres to Granada and what a sense of achievement we felt. We were beginning to get fed up with these mountains. Maybe we were just visiting them at the wrong time of year or maybe this was just freak weather, but whatever the reason we felt we had endured enough of the cold and wet. Once the visit to Granada was over we were coming to the conclusion we should change the route and escape to the coast. We reached Granada again in the rain and it made an inauspicious start to our visit. Along the N342 on the way into the city, we passed two campsites but we were hoping to find one closer to the city. However we looked in at the second; it was awful, very scruffy and with a dirty ablutions block – not where we wanted to spend the next few nights. We thought we would search on the main road to the south but when we reached that road, it turned out to be one of those forbidding bicycles. Now damp and cold and feeling just a little despondent we headed towards the city centre to look for a tourist information office – we found it – closed. However attached to the office was a sign, Camping Reina Isabella five kilometres. With the signs before us, we rode through the city centre, through all the traffic, the one-way system, and out the other side into the countryside, to a suburb called La Zuba.

What a lovely contrast to the site we had looked at an hour before. Though seemingly cramped this site was very efficiently run, had a well stocked shop and clean ablutions. The site was staffed by a young German couple who directed us to a pitch in 'Cyclist's Corner'. There were already two cyclists with minute tents when we arrived, and later in the afternoon we were joined by a Dutch couple and another German couple.

Chapter 6 Granada

We were so relieved to have reached Granada. This had probably been the toughest section of the journey but determination can be a great spur. Granada was one of the few cities we really wanted to see, a city with a tremendous history, the city of Castillian and Aragonese royalty and of conflicts, most notably with the Moors. I was hoping our visit to the Alhambra Palace would be memorable. It had taken four days of gruelling riding to cover the two hundred and fifty kilometres between Gibraltar and Granada; 'from the Rock to the hard places' and we felt justly proud of ourselves and, more importantly, our bicycles. We had just come through a week, Saturday to Saturday, of the most atrocious weather we could have envisaged. We had survived a nasty incident with Peter's blow-out. It could so easily have had terminal results (terminal as far as the expedition was concerned); more worryingly, it could also have caused him injury, so we felt we were being looked after yet again. Our escape from the mountains was fast becoming a reality and the final decision would be made over the weekend. Although we did not realise it at the time, we were approaching the half-way point of the expedition, 2365 kilometres covered, and we must have been extremely fit, but as on reaching this point, all we felt like was the few days rest which we awarded ourselves.

On the following morning we realised that Granada in early May was not as warm as we had hoped it would be, as the snow-covered Sierra Nevada mountains were between us and the sea. Still feeling the chill of altitude, we donned our jackets and caught the bus into the city to see the sights. In the centre we changed to another very crowded and ramshackle bus to climb the hill to the Alhambra Palace; it would have been pleasanter to walk but we did not know the way. The palace sits high up overlooking the city, an imposing position as we expected. In its heyday it must have been a most luxurious palace. We saw it partly preserved amongst shaded and well watered gardens, a peaceful place to spend part of a day well away from traffic and noise. It was just a little disappointing to find none of the rooms furnished as we had come to expect from our National Trust properties at home. Sometimes we were apt to forget we were abroad. The architecture of the palace is stunning, the Moorish plaster work like sugar icing on a wedding cake and colourful tiles decorating walls and floors. Closing one's eyes, it was easy to imagine elegantly dressed people of the 16th century gliding along the passages.

The gardens were laid out as a refuge from the summer heat, shade everywhere with little streams and channels connecting various pools, many with fountains. The Court of Lions had the best statuary but the other pools had more cooling fountains within the actual gardens. From the many vantage points, the views over the city and to the mountains were spectacular. Even though there were people entering all the time, we found many quiet spots in the gardens, one of which we chose to eat our picnic lunch undisturbed, except for a few sparrows who came for their share.

Instead of squeezing ourselves back onto the bus, we elected to walk back down into the city, not as far as we thought as we found a shortcut, and all downhill. We found the city centre full of colour. It was Fiesta weekend and the streets were full of women and girls of all ages (from pram size up) dressed in gorgeous flamenco dresses; all ruffles, frills and flowers in their hair. In the centre of a large square was a platform for dancing and it seemed anyone could go and join in. The dancers, mainly teenagers and toddlers, were thoroughly enjoying themselves. There were stalls selling black paper hats for the men who wanted to look the part, as well as the usual stalls with sweets and carnival goodies. We were also most impressed by processions of costumed horses and riders parading up and down the streets, it all looked very spontaneous.

By mid-afternoon our feet had had enough, so we found the bus back to La Zuba and spent the remainder of the afternoon in the sun which had now appeared. It was then we met an Australian couple, Dave and Kay, who with their teenage son, were travelling through Europe in an old English motor caravan. They loaned us two folding chairs and invited us to spend the evening with them after our meal in the restaurant. We must be exceedingly fussy as most of our meals eaten out were a disappointment and this was no exception, though it was lovely to have someone else to do the preparation. We had a most interesting evening chatting to our new friends, they were also expecting to go to Italy but would be there well before us. After leaving the Australians, we joined the cyclists round the candle-on-a-crate (instead of camp fire) in our 'corner' and finished off the evening with a bottle of wine (or few). They were very considerate and spoke in English for our benefit, most were spending a few weeks in Spain, but the Dutch had already been to Tangiers.

Having had two nights rest at this pleasant site, we decided it was time to discuss the feasibility of the route. Getting out the map, we looked at the pros and cons of our next planned stage, which was a direct mountain road to Murcia, a 278 kilometre run. Sitting at the campsite, we could see the mountain range which we would pass through was snow covered. Also, according to the map, something we had not taken into consideration before, there was a mountain pass of 1390 metres. These two factors were now combined with our experience of the last week. It was a foregone conclusion, so the next decision to make was which direction to make our escape. Looking at the map, there are five main roads out of Granada. We had ruled out the east one, we had come in on the west one, the two to the north were over more mountains so that left the southerly road, the N323, sixty-four kilometres to the coast at Motril, just skirting the Sierra Nevada. This road also had a pass, but only 860 metres, 530 metres lower than our first plan and well below the snow line. We knew it would be only a one day ride to the coast and we felt confident it would be a great deal warmer at sea level. We expected to find more traffic along the coastal strip but if we found it too much to cope with, the map showed we could escape inland a few miles and find peace. Trying to keep so far clear of the coast this time of the year had proved an uncomfortable experience.

We made our final bus visit into Granada to do some shopping. We were in need of a new gas cylinder for our lamp and I so wanted to see the Cathedral. Unfortunately we arrived just too late to see it as we had not realised that some sights close for siesta (for three hours). We could not find the right gas cylinder but did manage to find a candle! We also had a lazy walk round, with a quiet lunch in a shaded square, where the costumed citizens were still walking or riding about.

Our Dutch neighbours had spent an energetic day in the Sierra Nevada looking for snow which they found in plenty; whereas the Germans on our other side had spent a lazy day like us and were planning to visit the Alhambra the next day. After nearly three days in one place we had begun to feel restless, the need to move on was taking over as we prepared for a reasonably early start on the

Tuesday. There had been much coming and going on the site, all the more noticeable because of its small size. On our after-supper walk, the sun and clouds were in the right position for us to see the snow-clad mountains more clearly, and they looked very close.

(Top) Camp site at Caminha, Portugal - on arrival at a camp site we tended to 'explode'; our panniers, bikes and tent became makeshift washing lines.

(Bottom) Tarifa, Spain - mountain pass before Gibraltar, still reeling from the previous night's thunderstorm; forest of wind turbines in the background.

(Top)   Gibraltar - Sheila in conversation with a Rock Ape.

(Bottom)   Spanish coastal road near Mojacar - looking back on the hairpin climb we had just negotiated, not recommended for late afternoon on a hot sunny day.

(Top)   Valencia by-pass - the herd of armour-plated goats sculpture.

(Bottom)   Frontier crossing - Peter rides from Spain to France after breakfast before the traffic got there.

(Top) Provencale hillside - the most memorable wild camp site near Salon de Provence, France.

(Bottom) Peter saying farewell to Igoumenitsa en route for the airport and home.

Chapter 9 Escape from the Mountains

Although it had rained during the night, Tuesday 4th May dawned fair enough for us to start our escape and by nine o'clock, we had said farewell to our 'United Nations' of new friends at the Reina Isabella and pedalled out of the gates to look for the road south to the coast. We had a really beautiful day and were surrounded by some of the most lovely scenery once we had left the city environs. The N323 to Motril was a bit elusive for the first fifteen kilometres of the day but by using a parallel side road which we found accidentally we actually managed to miss the Passo del Suspiro Moro and soon found ourselves on the C323. We hoped it might be downhill all the way, and before Padul we were speeding down beside snow-covered peaks, which were retreating, much to our relief. Once we reached the valley of the Rio Guadalfeo, the winds were funnelling up at us and making our speed seem even faster and a bit dangerous. It was hard on the brakes and remembering the road to Loja, it seemed safer to dismount and walk down. This was reinforced when we saw, at a corner, the aftermath of an accident. The car may have been hit by a gust of wind which could have blown it against and almost under a lorry. Only the vehicles were there so it must have occurred some time before, but the winds were still very strong.

All the time we could feel a relaxing of the temperature as we dropped nearer to the sea and the scenery was that of deep canyons and gorges cut by the river whose valley we were following. Near Beznar the map showed a dam holding up a lake for supplying water to the area, we could not see the dam but parts of the lake were visible. Having left behind the snow and damp our spirits were much higher. Shortly after we had passed a spectacularly deep stretch of canyon that we estimated to be about eighty metres high, we felt it was time for a beer at the roadside café. The road was really living up to its green (scenic) designation, a breathtaking vertical cliff face was towering above the road. We felt highly exhilarated by our downhill ride of the morning and needed to stop to unwind a little before turning onto the coast road towards Motril. Circumstances had found for us a road to be highly recommended.

Close to where the river enters the sea we turned east onto the N340 and there was a complete change of scene. Gone were the hills and the lovely wild open countryside and in their place, banana groves giving way to urbanisation and industrialisation, interspersed with acres of plastic green-houses for tomatoes and fruit. The afternoon wind, when it arose was, of course, a headwind. The road was almost flat but it became a struggle, so after our lunch stop we carried on only another six kilometres before taking note of the sign that said there was a site another six further on. I found it so much easier to battle against a headwind when I knew for how much further I had to do battle; even though those six kilometres were uphill, past a lighthouse and through a tunnel. There was the site – 'Don Cactus', a vast area of caravan storage with a few spaces in between for us and another family to pitch our tents. Part of the fun of this expedition were the contrasts experienced within each day. This was a totally different area, the contrast between the mountains and the coast, an old city and a modern coastal resort and all within the ninety kilometres we had cycled that day. Coming off the mountains, we had passed the 1500 mile point, and hoped we had left the inclement weather behind.

Just as we settled down for the night, there was a thunderstorm and we realised the wind had turned into another wet rainstorm. Perhaps the area needed it but we thought we had left the mountains to escape from the rain. Were we wrong? Don Cactus was a site on sand and gravel, we had not realised we should have searched for boulders to weigh down our tent pegs. They had seemed firm enough at the time of pitching but during the night the concrete-like soil into which we hammered the pegs turned into wet cement. We woke before dawn to find the edges of our wet inner tent wrapping itself round our bodies and by now wet sleeping bags. Another lesson learned, followed by a day of enforced rest and drying out. Fortunately the empty site meant there was plenty of space in the large ablutions block where we could spread the sleeping bags, air mattresses and clothes over the stalls to dry, while we searched for boulders to place where we should have put them the previous night.

The nearest town was Calahonda, a couple of kilometres away, which we found later in the day once the rain had eased. Walking up between the tomato houses and the beach we found another ghost town of empty holiday apartments overlooking the empty beach with its leaning Martello-type tower. To keep our spirits up, we treated ourselves to a seafood supper made with some tinned octopus.

The best thing about all the storms we had encountered so far was that they did not last. A wet day was usually (hopefully) followed by a gloriously sunny one which made it so much easier to disregard the discomforts. The day which saw us depart from Don Cactus started with a glorious sunrise and we were soon moving eastwards along the coast road with its switchback contours. It was quite hard work cycling along it and we were imagining the task faced by those who had built the road. Hills dropping almost into the sea, cliff-sides to cling to and in places tunnels to be constructed. We followed this road faithfully to El Ejida just beyond which we found the junction with a road which would take us to the south of Almeria. The junction provided the only trees we had seen that day making an ideal spot for a restful lunch, but what a long hot afternoon. The minor road, though level, had no shade, no trees, almost no vegetation at all and until late in the afternoon, no campsites. Finally we came to Aquadulce which was a rather upmarket site, large separate pitches with awnings and palm trees. Our little tent and bikes looked a bit lost in a space for a caravan and car but who were we to complain? On our way to find food in the evening we came across a huge herd of multicoloured goats and narrowly missed being mixed up with them.

After Almeria we turned northeast and entered the film-set country through a desert which looked as if John Wayne and company could come riding along at any minute. Why did we think the Costas of Spain would be continuous high rise hotels when we were cycling across deserts? These deserts were interspersed with dramatic sections of coast road, by dramatic I mean steep. What wonderful wild and open scenery, not at all what I had expected, a real eye-opener! We were still trying to keep close to the coast whilst using reasonable roads which were not too crowded, yes we were really fussy about our ideal conditions. Although many of the roads we were following were marked on the map with a green line, denoting scenic route, some of the others should have been. The section before Mojacar was especially notable, although unfortunately reached near the end of a long hot day's riding. The road climbed very steeply up the side of a cliff, zigzagging way up above us. We could see what looked like the road after some climbing but it was (or looked) impossibly high above us. It must have taken well over an hour to climb the cliff, but the view from the top was incredible. It was satisfying to see from our vantage point the miniature cars and lorries starting the ascent. We discovered that the best thing about these steep climbs is that there is so often a bar at the top and with no hesitation, two large cold beers were soon on their way down to refresh the parts that were in need.

The site at Mojacar was the first reached after clocking the ton, 100.68 kilometres and what a day, culminating in that climb! It was at Mojacar that we met the Dutch baker and his Spanish wife cycling around this part of Spain looking for a town in which to settle and set up a bakery. We spent an interesting couple of hours swapping cycling experiences and they ended up giving us a larger scale map which was far better at showing cycle-friendly roads and more importantly, campsites. Ever after we tried to get maps of this scale! It meant more to carry but helped us a great deal.

Nearly twenty-four hours later we met Bill. While we were having our post-lunch relaxation we saw a heavily-laden cyclist of mature years pedalling up the hill we had just walked. He was too busy concentrating to see us but later when we arrived at our site there he was sitting outside his tent looking very relaxed as we staggered in to pitch near him. Bill is a Dutchman who takes a month every year to cycle-camp various parts of Europe on his own with a sophisticated mountain bike and lightweight equipment. He said he thoroughly enjoys his own company but is always happy to find a site where he can meet and talk to other people, especially cyclists. He told us he was sixty-three and had been doing this for several years since retiring. His wife does not like his type of cycling and prefers to holiday with relatives. Before leaving the next morning he took photos of us and gave us a loo roll; a pack of four was too bulky to carry!

After leaving Aguelas, our N332 turned inland to go behind the hills and gave us a tiring morning of gradual climbing into the wind. I was glad it was the right end of the day; it would not have been very funny had it been afternoon. Once behind the hills we turned east and had a lovely run down to Puerto de Marazon through some once again wild scenery, a little reminiscent of our moorlands at home though much warmer. The birdsong and empty roads made for relaxing cycling after the long pull up. This was repeated the following day to Cartagena as we had a long pull up and a much longer fast descent to the town.

Cartagena was a difficult town to cycle through although the town itself was fairly interesting. A naval port adjacent to an old walled town, it probably had a history worth exploring, but we met it too early in the day for a halt. The signs to Alicante were far too elusive, all the signs were for Murcia which was much too large a town for us. In fact we had to circle the town twice before finding someone who could give us directions which we could make sense of and find the right road. The silly thing was we wanted the continuation of the N332 but could not find it through the town. Once back on the right road, we followed it alongside a narrow little railway until La Union.

For the rest of the coast road towards Benidorm we had the wind pushing us along at a great rate. We were now getting towards the end of an eight day week and going well, not really tired at all. We had not found anywhere we liked enough to spend a 'weekend'. The facilities at the sites varied greatly and each day we had to keep going to find one as this part of the country was not suited to wild camping. This was a holiday area and although we came across much wild and open country, it was too open – there was very little cover to hide even a small tent. Sites were fairly plentiful, we really appreciated being able to have a shower at the end of a hot day's riding. Many of the open spaces were on the beaches and we felt that although not specifically forbidden in many areas, beach camping would probably have been unpopular if not rather risky.

After eight days continually on the go we had just 'rounded the corner' where the coast juts out towards the Balearics, the farthest point called Cabo de la Nao, but we had never heard of it either. We were pleased the motorway was running parallel to us all the way up this coast as it took much of the fast traffic away from us. Many times we were amazed at just how empty the roads were. We rode into Playa de Oliva just before the early afternoon thunderstorm which we could see approaching. There were so many campsites we were spoilt for choice, which is why the thunderstorm caught up with us. We had gone into the second site we saw for a look and to have lunch, but decided it was not right for a two day stay, so after eating we moved on to another.

All the mountain ranges seemed to sweep towards that corner of Spain, sending their wet clouds to follow us. We had been through a few light showers during the morning but just as this heavier one was starting, it was up-tent-double-quick-and-dive-inside-until-it-was-over.

The camp was well sheltered by trees which kept the worst of the winds off us and very soon it was all over. Out came the sun along with all the other campers. We found we had pitched close to the ablutions block which formed the cross-roads where everyone met. They were mostly retired people including an English couple who lent us table and chairs. It was so nice when we were able to sit and dine in comfort; it also made playing backgammon and scrabble much easier.

Citrus groves freshly washed give off the most memorable scent and it is this that will be one of my most lasting memories of this part of Spain. Just a day's ride from Valencia (the orange capital of the world?) and we found everywhere the trees with flowers and fruit in profusion. It must have been at this stage we realised I was the fruit freak, I just could not resist buying as much fruit as we could carry. It may have been a subconscious need for vitamin C, but it was the taste of the fresh fruit I found totally irresistible. I continued in this manner until the last day in Greece, when I was consuming fresh apricots as if they were going out of fashion; Peter just said he thought I must be pregnant!

After our rest day at Playa de Oliva, which we spent walking along the beach, relaxing and chatting with other campers, we set out to try and get past Valencia. The first town of the day was Gardia which I remember for its lovely treacle-toffee smell, combined with that of fresh-baked bread from the bakery we passed. As we cycled out of the town we were passed by a lorry carrying orange pulp, this must have been a 'nose important' day. The next town was obviously Cuillera, the name was in twenty to thirty foot high letters on the hillside! Then we were into the area of paddy-fields, which was confirmed by the signs stating they belonged to 'Arroz-Sud', the brand name on the packets of rice we had been buying. Heading for Sueca which on the map was designated a town with a campsite but of it we saw neither sight nor sign. We reached Sueca far too early in the day to go searching for a site, so we carried on. However, by mid-afternoon we became concerned that we were getting too close to Valencia and not finding the bypass. We were sure we were on the right road and had been looking for the bypass ever since lunch. Either we had misread the map or the road layout had changed since the map was printed, but the countdown was advancing towards the city. We had to decide either to 'retrace our pedals' or to cut across country and try to pick up the road. Of course we chose the more adventurous way, to the town of Torrent and then towards Montserrat, all the time realising it was going to mean a night of camping wild if we could find anywhere suitable.

Belatedly we found the bypass but we were then very tired and disgruntled, but lucky enough to find a delightful pitch between two orange groves just a short distance off the main road. Stony ground again but right up against a wall bordering one of the orchards. I admit we did succumb; the forbidden fruit lived up to its reputation, sweet and so juicy, doubly delicious.

Valencia bypass will be remembered for its sculptures; to make the road more interesting the Spanish have placed at intervals some roadside sculptures. After about an hour's riding along the level and fairly empty road we came across, about half a kilometre away, a herd of goats grazing the verge. They looked a little out of place but we had come to expect the unexpected. They did not even move as we got closer and there seemed to be no-one looking after them. No wonder, they were made out of plate steel, painted black and white, about fifty of them. After another hour of travel along this road we saw another herd and just before we left the bypass to turn off to Borriana we saw a rainbow standing at least thirty feet high made of steel piping and gaily painted.

After leaving the bypass we began to be passed by the weekend 'Tour de France' types. Several groups of brightly dressed and cheerily waving cyclists seemed to be coming from Castellon, where we thought there must a big cycle racing club. There always seemed to be riders out at weekends – it must be a very popular sport. The site at Borriana was extensive and of well-watered grass but had the disadvantage of no drinking water on site. They offered to sell us a bottle at the bar but at such an exorbitant price that we bought a great five litre bottle in the town later. However, there were lovely hot showers, once one had mastered the eccentricities of the taps. The showers provided the afternoon's entertainment. We were most amused to watch our nearby tent neighbours going for their showers; first she went escorted by him and they soon returned with her wrapped in the enormous pink towel and him carrying everything. Soon after they set off again together, he with towel around his neck and her as escort only to return within a short while with him wrapped in the enormous pink towel and her as escort. Soon after their washing line was adorned with the towel and two sets of smalls.

From Castellon to Barcelona took us four days of hard pedalling covering distances of over eighty-five kilometres on each of the first three. By this time we had settled into a routine of covering as much distance before lunch as possible, spending an hour or so over the lunch break and mini-siesta before finishing the day's riding, hoping to find a site by mid-afternoon. We were having a fairly puncture-free time after having left the mountains and replacing both our rear tyres, strangely enough the fronts were showing no signs of wear but the rear ones were carrying most of the weight. In fact, my front one is still in place after a further thousand miles after returning home!

Castellon, though fairly large as towns go, was traversed early on a Sunday morning, the best time of the week to meet a town. As there were neither traffic nor directional problems, it was delightfully easy. However, once out in the country with other cyclists whizzing past, we wondered whether the lorries were not having a Sunday that week, as there were so many of them about. The wind had turned and was no longer favouring us but we still made good progress and reached the outskirts of Vinaros in plenty of time to find a site. 'Ants under Mulberry Trees' we called this one, a very attractive setting, but no escaping the ants which did nip. Unfortunately we could not persuade the owner to open his site shop as it was 'family fiesta' so we had to use the emergency meal bought in Gibraltar without wine. This was a hardship; we had told ourselves all along we needed the iron the red wine provided. So convincing had we been that I do not think a day had gone by when we had not taken our advice. Usually packed in Tetra-Brik cartons which had made it easily transportable, there was really no excuse not to imbibe. That night we had to make do with the open bar, where the assistant barman served very generous tots of gin and martini.

Vinaros provided an excellent supermarket for stocking up but I was very upset by the sight and smell of the pig lorries which passed us on the way through the town. Several slatted sided lorries containing barely alive pigs obviously en route for slaughter, the animals crowded in inhumanely, piled on top of each other and the smell of fear was appalling. The things we humans do in order to feed our bellies; I am sure English pig producers are little better.

Tuesday, 18th May, almost the middle of the month, and we were about half way up the coast of Spain, marked by the delta of the Rio Ebro. This very large estuaried river flows from just south of our starting point at Santander right through Spain to a large delta system on the east coast. We had not crossed the river before but had taken nearly two months to get right round to it. If we decided to return by the route south of the Pyrenees, we expected to follow much of its length and valley, but that would be in another two months time. We crossed by the N340 which runs close to the motorway at this point, The crossing is by a large bridge close to cement works. It seemed that much of the delta is given over to paddy fields and we seemed to be making good progress bowling along at over thirty kph with the wind behind us. After L'Aidea we left the low ground and began to climb over moorland terrain. Our lunch stop at the edge of a field was surrounded by flowers mostly new to us; bright pink starlike flowers and red and blue pimpernels growing amongst stunted pine trees. We followed this moorland country road for another ten kilometres before returning to the coast beyond L'Hospitalet de L'Infant where we started to look for a site. We felt sure (and the map confirmed) that there would be sites along this coastal section but up till four o'clock, we had found none. Never mind, there was a good supermarket to stock up and inside it I found an English party doing the same, so I asked them if they could recommend a campsite. Of course it turned out they were caravanning on a large and luxurious site only ten minutes away, and it was one of a string of fifteen sites just on the other side of the hill.

Very thankfully we found the site. It was large and it was luxurious with facilities geared up for those who visit for a fortnight's holiday. Swimming pool, cinema, bar and restaurant, site shop and children's playgrounds, but we did use the swimming pool and it was most welcome. We even found hot washing-up water but were not warned about the 'night visitors'.

In the morning Peter woke up and immediately killed two mosquitoes remarking that they were full of blood. I knew they were, it was mine. I had been bitten on both eyelids; I had holdalls over my eyes and could hardly see out, so I was very uncomfortable for the first part of the day until the swellings had gone down. Otherwise the site had been excellent; one of the cheapest in this area and definitely the best value.

As we cycled past Salou, the place where Peter had spent his first holiday in Spain, we could see the high-rise hotels, but he did not want to divert and revisit it. Instead we made an unusual decision, to go into Tarragona. We had been trying to avoid towns when at all possible but here we were, actually heading into the centre of one, because we wanted to find a good bookshop which would provide a large scale map of the next section of the country. Luckily Tarragona not only supplied the map but had some excellent sign posting. We found the book shop by going to a travel agent. They did not have the map but they gave us a street plan with bookshops clearly marked and the first of these had what we wanted.

Tarragona was only a day's cycling away from Barcelona, which was to be one of the most stressful cities we went through. We had spent the previous night at Sitges in a site overlooked by some high-rise flats. We had awoken to a thunderstorm that morning but had not seen it as an omen – we just took a little longer to get moving and by the time we left camp the skies had cleared.

The journey to the outskirts of the city was a pleasant one; up and down the cliff roads, it was scenic and not busy. I had been rather startled by a huge black snake about five feet long which had been alarmed by my bike and scuttled out of my way, I had never seen anything that size before. Previously we had seen signs to the Tunnels of Garaf and on our ride that morning we saw them. They turned out to be tunnels containing the motorway so that it did not have to follow the cliffside road up and down as we did. We felt quite sorry for the drivers speeding along out of sight of the scenery we were enjoying. All they had was brief glimpses as they disappeared into their rocky tombs.

Once we reached Castelldefels, urbanisation took over and the assembling clouds began to dump dampness on us. The outskirts of the city caught up with us before mid-morning and did not let us go until well into the afternoon. Our street map was one for motorists who could travel along the length of the streets much quicker than we could and who preferably knew more or less where they were going. As we fitted into neither of these categories, we found it a bit more difficult to get through the city. We had hoped to find a campsite at Badelona, just beyond the city centre, but we could not tell where the city ended and the suburbs began. Barcelona itself was a maze of traffic lights with continuous traffic between them. I rode through, thinking that it could only be tackled by someone who is very brave or foolhardy or in the company of one who rides behind shouting at me to keep going. Shades of the Seville ring road, I know I had not felt so stressed since that day and this time it was raining as well. We had to use a fair bit of navigation-by-nose as most of the signs were for motorists wanting to use the motorway to Gerona. We did eventually get the hang of not getting on the motorway slip roads and found the N11 more by good luck than judgement. We did not realise we had been in Badelona until we were almost out of it and we had seen nothing resembling a campsite.

At least we were on the road we wanted to be on, even though it was a pretty awful experience. We pressed on towards Mataro hoping we would not have to pedal all that way. The N11 runs alongside the railway, which runs alongside the waterline, it is a straight and level road but far too narrow for the volume of traffic using it. Due to the absence of campsite signs and the fact that it was nearing mid-afternoon and we had had no lunch, I was almost in despair. At Montgap we suddenly saw (through the rain) a campsite on the opposite side of the road, but as we crossed and rode up to the gate, we realised it was closed. To get to it, we had been forced to cross the horrendously busy road which had taken a long time for a break in the stream of traffic. To get back on would mean crossing again and we could see no chance of a break, so we walked along the other side for nearly two kilometres before we could get back on track. Once we remounted, what should we see but another site and on the opposite side of the road...but this time it was open and what a relief.

Chapter 10   Barcelona to the Border

Nearly 3.30pm and our bellies were empty, so we lunched on the remains of our provisions before pitching the tent. This was only just achieved before the rain started again, so in we dived to collapse for a couple of hours before deciding on the next move. Considering how close this site was to such a busy road, it was remarkably peaceful. Had we not been so keen to visit Barcelona, we would have routed ourselves well away from the city, though it would have meant more mountains. As usual a bit of rest worked wonders and by early evening, Peter was ready to do some more maintenance on his bicycle. This time his front wheel bearings needed checking and re-greasing. After this we walked out to find a food shop and see about the train service into the city. We spoke to the German couple camped next to us, who said they had used the train successfully so we went over to the station and looked up the timetable. Trains appeared to be very frequent, and the station was close to the site.

The relative peace of the site was shattered by the arrival of the 'Sliding-door Germans', a couple with a caravanette which had the noisiest sliding doors we had ever heard and was parked very close to our tent. They seemed to start their breakfast before anyone else woke up which we guessed by the several times their door was opened and closed; they also made a great deal of metallic noise laying the table both mornings.

We decided to stay two nights so we could go into Barcelona for the day. The train service was the most convenient way to travel in from the suburbs. The railway ran from about twenty-five kilometres out of the city, stopping at each of the little towns along the way. The service was fast, smooth, frequent and above all clean. Just before it entered the city centre it became a metro and went below the streets with several stations from which one could emerge to see the sights. There was a VDU showing time, temperature and constant location. I was most impressed and felt that British Rail should follow this example and provide something similar between Plymouth and Exeter. We did however find walking round Barcelona very tiring – we were just not used to spending so long on our feet. We wanted to send a telegram to Peter's daughter who was getting married on Saturday, we wanted to find out about the ferries to and from Genoa and we wanted to see the Cathedral. The first was accomplished very easily, the post office counter staff were most helpful and persuaded us to send a fax which was faster, cheaper and more convenient. With the ferry offices we had no success, we tried several but could get no information at all. The Cathedral we found with the help of the post-office-supplied street map; the 14th century building was too dark and off-putting for our liking – all the chapels were enclosed (or rather shut-off) by railings. We only found one which was open for prayer. However, the stained glass was magnificent.

The Church of the Holy Family was totally different; this we really enjoyed, even though we could not go inside. In a different part of the city, it looked partly ruined as it was roofless. In fact it had been started in 1881 and never completed as the models were burnt in 1936. What we saw were great spires soaring up high above the walls with their scenes from the life of Christ in relief. The building appeared to be in the process of restoration (or even completion) but even the cranes could not detract from its elegance. It was not a very large church but we found it absolutely magnificent. Even the architecture looked light and airy, we just walked around in wonder looking at the reliefs and ate our lunch close by.

We needed our lunch to fuel our arduous afternoon. Following (so we thought) the street map, we walked back towards the station. We did not so much get lost, as have extreme difficulty finding the right street and we had almost walked out of the city before we gave up and hailed a taxi to take us back to the station. Of course we had passed very close to it in the course of our wanderings, so we were very tired when we returned to the site at four o'clock, again blessing the train service and its nearness to our site.

Back at the site we watched the comings and goings of our fellow campers. A young couple arrived on foot; we had seen very few of these hardy souls who carried their world on their backs. It certainly was not the way I would wish to travel; I was far happier to let the bike do the carrying even though my legs had to power it.

As we left Barcelona on the second morning, we regretted we had not enjoyed it as much as we had hoped. We had been warned about pickpockets but had kept our wallets under our shirts and had not felt threatened. Probably by this stage of the journey we had been put off towns and cities and therefore did not approach them with much enthusiasm. When we had planned the route, we had not had experience of much traffic so these cities had just been names on a map; places read about in history or travel books without knowing what they would really be like and how unsuited to cycle travel. In fact we realised how fortunate we had been not to meet with serious problems. Apart from my knock in Lugo, we had had no accidents with traffic, although the amount of it we had been amongst was tremendous. All in all we had been wonderfully protected and we prayed it would last.

Still heavily travelled, the N11 led us east away from Masnou and the Barcelona area. It was something of a slog along the coastal part as all the towns joined onto each other and the traffic was continuous until we reached Santa Susanna, where we turned north towards Gerona. Once away from the coast we found countryside again and how lovely it was. As we pedalled along that busy road we were so thankful we had found the site at Masnou; there had been no others for at least ten kilometres. The first one we passed that day had been one called Kangaroo; it was high up above the road so we could only guess how to reach it!

The only thing that marred the country road we cycled along in the middle of the day was the sight of yet more dead bodies. Sad little corpses mainly of cats which had been knocked down by speeding cars and left there to desiccate in the heat. It was our intention to miss Gerona and take the C253 to Llagostera, which the map showed as having a campsite. A minor road with almost English-looking hedges and fields, it was still green in mid-May. There was a delightful spot for lunch, down an old fashioned-looking lane, where we ate sitting under an ash tree, amongst the clover beside a small stream. We felt this was what our expedition was all about; we could hear no traffic; the silence was almost overwhelming after the last few days. We hoped to find something similar for our night's camp.

Now within our final couple of days in Spain, we had rounded our final 'corner' of the country during the morning. Before long, it seemed we would meet the French border at La Jonquera south of Perpignan. We spent a night at a deserted site some way out of Llagostera which had no more than a good nearby supermarket to recommend it. On these storage sites, there was hardly a soul about and the following morning we could not find anyone to take our fee so we pushed a 1000 peseta note through the door hoping that would be right. Along the road that day, we kept seeing the "Last chance to

Lloret" signs. Peter had holidayed at Lloret de Mar just before we met and had semi-suggested going via the town to see if it was the same. When I pointed out the signs he said he did not really want to go back, it had been all high-rise hotels and commercialism. He did not want to spoil the lovely scenery we were passing. This final part of Spain was very pretty and was preparing us for France where we were to see some lovely sights.

Our final night before crossing the border into France was at the frontier town of La Jonquera, which we found quite entertaining. We arrived at mid-afternoon and found the small site very empty. It was the first site at which we had been asked for payment on arrival. It was a very pleasant site, we had a pitch beside the river which only had the disadvantage of mosquitoes during the evening. We were to need our repellent almost wherever we found water from then on. The site was not nearly as noisy as we expected considering all the lorries which were queuing up along the road waiting to cross the frontier. It was an entertaining evening seeing all the nationalities waiting there. The whole town had an atmosphere of frontier, all the tourist shops (of which there were many, as day-tripping seems a popular occupation) showed two prices, as we had seen in Gibraltar. We were happy that the site backed onto a supermarket so we could stock up on some of our favourite Spanish dishes. Tomorrow would be a new country and shopping, as well as life, would once again be an adventure.

To travel through the second part of Spain had taken us thirty-two days, of which we had spent twenty-five nights on sites and only seven wild. Our cost of living had been £9.50 each per day at exchange rate of 160 pesetas to the pound. We had ridden 2074 very adventurous kilometres and we felt we had become used to Spain. We had enjoyed it immensely and would like to return with our bicycles at a later date.

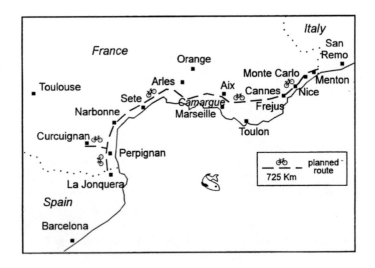

Chapter 11   Into France

Paying our site fee the previous day proved to be an advantage, for we could leave La Jonquera as early as we wanted. We said good-bye to our last and very comfortable site in Spain (we had even been provided with loo paper as well as hot water).

It only took a short time to realise the easiest way to cross the border is by bicycle, as we rode past all the stationary lorries and other vehicles rather smugly. The two border posts at La Jonquera, on the Spanish side and Le Perthus, on the French, were a few kilometres apart with a deserted 'no man's land' between. No delays and we were in France, green, wild and hilly. I had become pleasantly surprised at how easy it was to travel between countries in Europe, I suppose it is an advantage of the closer economic ties. The only disappointment was that it meant we were not able to collect stamps in our passports.

Sunday, 23rd May, and we reached Perpignan before elevenses, to be known as 'Jus-break'in France. Once again on well-surfaced roads and still parallel to motorway taking most of the traffic away from us. We sat opposite the airport at Perpignan to consume our *jus d'orange* and biscuits. In the centre of the town we found a bank which, although closed for Sunday, we were able to enter with our Visa card and draw French cash. We also looked for a petrol station to buy a map of a better scale for cycling. We had to look for a small village called Curcuignan where we hoped to meet our friends, Stella and Ben. It was a good thing we also bought food at the petrol station, this first day in France turned out to be a very hard one.

We tried twice more to phone our friends but decided the phone would not connect as the number must be incomplete. Having located Curcuignan, we made our way up there. Stella had told Peter it was in the mountains but we had not realised quite how steep these mountains were. We travelled up the valley of the River Maury noting the camp sign. We were now well and truly in wine country, vines as far as they eye could see and everywhere signs inviting "*vende et degustation*", which I translated roughly as "buy and try". As we left the villages and pedalled through the even more rural areas, we saw signs designating the ownership of the vineyards along with the now familiar "*Appellation Controllee*" signs. We stopped at the village of Maury for lunch which we ate at the side of an empty petanque pitch on one of the spectators' benches. It seemed to be rather cold but we were climbing. After lunch we left Maury heading north and straight up, yes it was to be an afternoon of hill climbing.

As it turned out, our visit to Curcuignan was wasted. Stella and Ben had flown into Perpignan on time but, as we later found out, had not yet reached their destination. They had been delayed over a mix up with their hire car and were at the time much nearer the airport. We had an arduous climb over the mountain to the village where we should have met them but fortunately it was absolutely beautiful. The hillsides so wild, undeveloped and carpeted with wild flowers, some familiar, some seldom seen, like pyramid orchids and others we did not know at all. We found the house easily enough but the conversation I had with the next door neighbour left us both totally confused. The owner of the house, an English lady called Anne, had gone off to England in January and had not informed him when she would return. In the meantime she had lent the house to our mutual friends, but the neighbour did not know when they were coming. Whatever the circumstances, the result was the same, they had not arrived. We later discovered they actually arrived twenty-four hours after we had been there to find our note. Unfortunately they had been carrying six spare inner tubes for us, a spare tyre and two jars of powdered tea. It was something of a loss to be without these but we would have to manage. If we had only known that we could have met them the following day, we would have stayed nearby.

As it was, there was nothing else to do but return towards Perpignan to find somewhere to camp; we had seen a sign at Estagel but that seemed a long way back and we discovered the site at Maury was closed. The castle of Quebus at the top of the mountain (built in 1000 AD) gave some panoramic views over this most picturesque of areas; no wonder Anne had chosen to retire here. What a trip back to Estagel! From Quebus it was almost all downhill on a truly glorious afternoon. The views had made the diversion worthwhile but it was a shame we were retracing the journey, a thing we never like to do.

The site at Estagel was our first experience of 'Sites Municipal', a town site with only very basic accommodation but very cheap. As it was just before the season opened, there was no fee. There was just a small patch of empty ground on the edge of the town with a small public conveniences block which consisted of two cold water taps, two flushing loos and a locked shower. We had some company, a party of about ten Dutch youngsters who were crammed into three tiny tents, but they were not as noisy as we feared they would be. Whilst cooking supper, I was called to look over to the north west to see what appeared to be the clouds on the distant hills. Of course it was really the snow on the thankfully distant Pyrenees – I was quite speechless, it was the third mountain range on which we had seen snow. We had just completed another day on which we had almost done the ton, 99.75 kilometres, a really hard day, and we felt we had covered a great deal of ground. Out of three planned meetings only one had been successful; now we were completely on our own, any more tea or inner tubes we might need, we would have to find for ourselves.

Estagel was a friendly little town and good for shopping. We followed our noses to the bakery in the morning and found it next to the grocery. Shopping was much easier in France, as I could recognise and say the names of things we wanted and felt more relaxed about my attempts at the language. We were heading north up the coast and looking forward to reaching Provence. We had been there some years previously on holiday with my parents although then we had been away from the coast, up in the mountains. Before Provence we were hoping for a 'weekend' at the Camargue.

The Camargue is an area with a fascinating sound to it; we had heard of the white horses and the area of marshland but knew nothing else. We did not yet know of the Mistral factor which we were to discover. Our second day in France was a complete contrast to the first – we spent most of it on a main road leading to Narbonne, a good flat road but with a strong headwind. We rode into the town looking for both a campsite and a supermarket. The latter was easily found, it was enormous, and all the locals were coming out with trolleys piled high with their necessities, whereas ours fitted into a small handbasket in order not to overload our panniers. However, we were surprised not to find a site and had to cycle on to the next town Cousan, where we found a scruffy and neglected site called 'The Oasis'. Sadly neglected, it had the potential to be really attractive. The pitches were all on grass with a few shady trees but everywhere there was rubble and litter and the ablutions block had an old cement mixer, half blocking the doorway.

This part of France was notable for its marvellous scent of broom flowers all along the roads, I'm sure we would have missed so much had we been on four wheels. Using the map we had bought near the border, we had an interesting morning map reading, to work our way around Beziers which looked like a town best avoided. Our route took us through such charming little villages, Nissan, Vendes and Seguir which all looked frozen in time. Narrow winding streets, so we could never be sure of the right direction, but with such character we didn't mind – we were having a very enjoyable morning's ride. We even passed a tiny aerodrome at the top of the hill above Vendes, just three light aircraft standing on the grass airstrip. Our mid-morning *jus* was taken on the canal-side path, originally the towpath, it had been partly surfaced and made into a cycle track. We could not follow it, as it was going the wrong way for us but it made a pleasant stopping place. There is something so peaceful about a canal, overhanging trees giving shade and coolness and the fish rising and making rings. We were quite reluctant to move on but we hoped to reach Sete for the night.

The tranquil part of the day was over as soon as we left the canal side. We made three attempts to get onto the N112 but each time were confronted with the "No Bicycles" sign. We asked a few passers by and even a gendarme for directions to Sete. I was trying to explain that we needed a road on which the bikes would be allowed, but obviously my French was incorrect, I just met plenty of Gallic shrugs. However we finally found a sign that put us onto the right road and led us to the N112. Once on this road it was long, straight and busy and we made good progress. This day we saw the first pair of bee-eaters, brilliantly electric blue birds that flew over the road and away into the bushes; so good to see a live pair after the sad little body I had seen in Spain.

Before midday, we were riding along the sand bar which encloses the Thau basin, eighteen kilometres long and on the seaward side all golden beach with not a single ice-cream van in sight. We lunched amongst the dunes and even paddled in the sea but it was too hot to have a siesta with no shade. Less than an hour after our lunch stop, we entered Sete and found another Site Municipal most conveniently in the town. We then realised our final weeks in Spain had spoilt us for sites as this was again basic and had no trees and therefore no shade. A small, completely walled area, where, after dark, two enormous iron gates were pulled across the entrance and we were definitely in for the night! It was well placed for the town's facilities, only a short walk to the shops where, before re-provisioning, we enjoyed a beer, long, cold, expensive but most appreciated. We replaced the footpump for the airbeds, as ours had finally given up. I also had to make pannier repairs that evening, the stitching needed periodic repairs but this time a side zip had parted company with the slider disappearing, so I had to put on a button and shoelace-loop. In Sete we bought our first phonecard which made talking to those at home easier; we had been finding so many card-only phone booths the farther south we had come.

The evening entertainment was provided by two American girls putting up their tent. They each had their own idea of how it should be done but the ideas did not coincide. The result was much like the Victoria Wood TV programme we had seen; framework being put together then taken apart again, bits being put up and then taken down. They did eventually get it all together before making an exit for a well-earned drink, I am sure they wish they had practised in privacy first. Last thing at night before turning in was to see the Chinese woman in charge of the site, locking grilles over the washroom entrances; we hoped we would not get caught short during the night.

The way out of Sete was reminiscent of Plymouth harbour, the road taking us all round by the quayside to follow the signs to Montpellier, back onto the very windswept N112. The N112 was to take us along the coast, through the Petit Camargue and then to the Camargue proper. Our French map showed the Camargue as being basically the delta of the river Rhone, a flat area extending from Montpellier in the west to near Marseilles in the east. There are several enclosed salt water lakes, large areas of marshland and few roads. We were unused to seeing land so flat and the roads we were on did not afford any views – we could only see the area immediately surrounding the road. In order to really explore the Camargue properly, one would need to hire a horse.

It was on one of the Etangs (sand-bar enclosed lakes) that we saw our first flamingos. We had to stop and take another look, as we were so amazed to see these large pink birds wild and so close. A little farther on we saw our first Camargue horses, which reminded me of Irish Connemaras, being similar in size and colour. Most of the sturdy little horses we saw on the Camargue proper were tethered, waiting to give rides to tourists and looking very hot and bored.

We found a few kilometres of cycle track which were between Pavelas and Carnon, quite unusual. Close to Aigues-Mortes

94

(translatable as dead leaves I believe), we turned south to head for Saintes-Maries-de-la-Mer which appeared to be the only town and at the end of the road. It was at the turn we met the full force of the wind which was blowing from where we wanted to go. After a bit of struggle we found a welcome picnic place with tables and benches; most convenient to lean the bikes up against, while we changed a punctured tube – the first for some time. We had to keep a tight hold onto our bread and cheese as the wind was becoming so fierce. Although it was a south wind, it was quite cool so we did not linger as we wanted to get on and find the site.

There followed almost another twenty kilometres of very hard work; on any other day (without wind) it would have been a cyclist's paradise. Lovely flat wide roads with no towns and hardly any traffic. It was just the wind, all the way along that lovely straight flat road, that slowed us down so we were creeping along in lowest gears at about 9 kph. We were so happy to see the Clos de Rhone campsite on the outskirts of Saintes-Maries. It looked very upmarket for us scruffy cyclists but by that time we were past caring. It was very expensive but we needed two comfortable nights, so we cheerfully entered and pitched with our backs to the wind. We had seen other cyclists that day mostly going in the opposite (sensible) direction, but as we arrived, a lone cyclist rode in, who was meeting up with a companion who had already arrived. During the evening we were treated to the sight of another cycling couple arriving, one of whom was towing a small bike trailer. We found this very interesting as the previous summer we had tried to build a trailer for our tandem which had not been a success. This trailer was small, looked very light and seemed to tow perfectly. However, when we went to look for them for a chat after our meal, their tent was deserted, they must have gone into the town for supper.

This was the first site we had been on that had mixed ablution blocks (fortunately in cubicles), which I found a bit disconcerting the first time I came out of the shower. I was delighted to find warm water for washing clothes and dishes but I managed to lose another plug. We had actually reached the Camargue to have a 'weekend' at the end of one of our cycling weeks, arriving on a Wednesday evening. Our calculations showed we had cycled 527 kilometres in the last week, one of our highest weekly totals. We had passed the 4,000 mark that day, had been travelling for nine weeks and with to date, only ten rest days. I think we had good reason to be proud of our achievements so far and we were about to make our eleventh puncture repair! We blessed Peter's foresight in carrying enough inner tubes to make roadside changes so that repairs could be carried out later. Not having the expected extra tubes, we prayed our stock would last. Apart from the seemingly major problems with both our rear wheels, the brake set replacement and stripping the wheel bearings, our maintenance schedule had been surprisingly light and we still had a good supply of spare cables and blocks.

At 8am, I dutifully went to the site shop and secretly bought four croissants as a treat for our breakfast. Only the French can make them so light and mouth-watering and we had come a long way for such a treat. Deciding to be holidaymakers for the day, we cycled into the town to find it as we expected, a tourist town well-populated with tourists. I caught sight of a man carrying an English paper, so I asked him where the English paper shop was, and we bought a daily that was only two days old. We had not read any news since Granada but we enjoyed being out of touch. The town was full of shops selling take-away foods as well as a marvellous *boulangerie*, so for the second time in only a few hours I succumbed and bought two calorie-filled goodies for our 'Sunday Tea'. We found the supermarkets were catering for the 'apartment tourists' and were quite expensive for our provisions, but the wine did come in one and a half litre bottles (imported from Spain!).

The wind blew strongly all of our rest day at Clos du Rhone which made drying the laundry a quick job. It also gave us a half-hour's amusement as we watched a pair of girls in high heels trying to fold up their tent against the wind. They looked so out of place, teetering around in their unsuitable shoes with their tent filling up with wind and refusing to shrink to fit its bag, we wondered whether France was to be peopled with entertaining campers. Peter deprecatingly remarked "Just like women to try to fold their tent into the wind", but he did not offer to help them – he was too busy laughing. We spent a lovely hour or so in the site pool, it was sheltered from the wind and we had it to ourselves. We had found so few sites with pools and I was determined to get full value out of this very expensive one. Having had such luxurious food during that day, we even expanded our culinary skills to cooking real potatoes. Sliced thinly they cooked quickly and did not use up too much of our precious gas. We also had lovely fresh peaches for dessert, I suppose we had become so food-conscious because most of our shopping was for our stomachs, our limited facilities made any variety an achievement.

Friday, 28th May, saw us on the move again. During the night the wind had dropped but with the dawn had risen again, this time in the opposite direction, which meant we had to start against a headwind. As we paid up, the site receptionist mentioned the Mistral, thus confirming my suspicions. For the first twelve kilometres we struggled into the wind, before changing direction towards Arles. Alongside the Petit Rhone we stopped to photograph a Camargue mare and foal in a field close to the road. Once we had joined the N570, with the wind behind us, we really bowled along, happy at last not to be fighting it and able to enjoy the scenery! Overhead flew a large flock of birds which we thought and hoped must have been flamingos.

Near to Arles we came up against a French problem we were to find a few more times before we crossed into Italy. It seemed that around many of the towns the 'through' routes have been upgraded to motorway status, thus forbidding bicycles. This makes navigation very confusing for the humble cyclist who does not really wish to go into the town just in order to find a sign to get out again. We had been trying to regain the N113 which should take us to Aix-en-Provence, but it was not easy. However on this occasion the problem was to be a bonus, after asking directions a few times we found ourselves on a delightful road to St Martin. This was a small town full of street market stalls just packing up and we had to dodge the stallholders carrying the remains of their produce back to their vans, as well as various barriers and a smiling gendarme.

At Arles it seemed that at last we had entered that delightful area, Provence. The road we were on, the alternative to the N113, was the typical Provençale road one sees in paintings; fairly straight, tree-lined and comfortably without gradients. Beside us were small fields mostly cut for hay and overhead we could hear and see hawks. With the wind behind us, partly shaded from the sun by trees, we were making excellent progress and really enjoying yet another day of complete contrast. Just before lunch we met up with the N113, by now much narrower and we were alarmed to read a sign stating "25 accidents in 1992".

This was one of our best and most scenic days. The perfect end to such a day was the wild site we inadvertently found on a Provençale hillside. A short distance out of Salon de Provence, (where we had only just found a food shop and failed to find an official site despite hopefully following a sign), we left the road and pushed up a green lane. There we found a gap that led out onto open ground, stony but with low-growing rosemary and thyme bushes amongst small bushy pine trees. A quarter of an hour to clear away all the stones from an area large enough for our small tent, a tussle with the ants who declared they were there first and we had a perfect haven for the night. We shall always remember our 'Hillside in Provence' – the scent of wild herbs was intoxicating, the views across the countryside uninterrupted and the sunset surpassed, even the one we had seen in Portugal with our friends. By 6.30pm we had pitched the tent, the air was incredibly clear and we could easily understand why this area had been chosen by artists for its wonderful light. We ate our supper and drank the evening bottle of wine watching the sun sink from an amazingly colourful sky. The only regret was that our camera was unable to capture the incredible colours. The sun dropped like a burnished globe behind the blue hills as the lights of a distant town attempted to replace it.

At sunrise we were greeted with the same views with the fresh clear morning air and again the art-inspiring light of Provence. The scent of the herbs was with us as we wheeled back to the road regretfully. We would like to have stayed longer just to soak up the atmosphere, but Aix-en-Provence and beyond were calling. This, the most memorable of our wild sites, will remain with us for a long, long time. Making our way down to the road, we noticed that the pink rockroses had come into flower since our arrival the previous evening. They were lining the road like flags and there were numerous white speckled butterflies all about us. Quickly finding the D10 to Aix, we stopped at the prettily-named village of La Feu les Oliviers to buy provisions including some most appetising smelling bread. French loaves are undoubtedly at their best in their country of origin and we were finding some beauties. The girl in the bakery to whom I chatted said we were "tres courageux" and wished us "Bon Voyage".

Thirty kilometres of countryside to Aix and as we neared the town the Mont St Victoire came into view, Cézanne's personal mountain which featured in so many of his paintings. We had seen it when in the area seven years before, but had not remembered it as being so close to Aix. We did however remember the fields of poppies which lined the roads that morning. Only the fields of lavender were missing, they were further north. Close to Aix we made another of those useful finds that were to our benefit. Our plastic sheet that we had found at Santiago had fast been wearing out, had it been a little larger it would have been a bit more useful. Just below an embankment, Peter spotted a large piece of blue replacement sheeting. This was big enough to give us not only a piece to cover the bikes at night and ourselves during any unexpected rainshower, but a second piece he cut to use in the tent entrance which would keep the inside of the tent cleaner. We had not realised before we left that this would become an essential piece of the camping equipment.

Aix was one of those towns that was easy to navigate through and we only had to ask directions once, this time to St Maxime. It was an area of delicate harebells alternating with brilliant poppies. After Aix we tried to find a view of the Mont St Victoire to photograph but we were out of luck. Instead we followed along a cliff face of vertical limestone that presented itself to the camera. It seemed like a good idea to stop and give in to the tempting loaf for lunch, before stocking up again later on in the afternoon. We had just realised we were facing a bank holiday weekend. We had no idea of French shop opening policy and we had no wish to be caught-out so we bought a little extra.

Our last night in Provence was spent at a wild site beside a river in the company of the biggest mosquitoes we had ever seen, all wearing their black and gold football jerseys. They first found me when I had stripped off to wash in the river, which meant I had to have a quick splash and cover up again. It was so good to find a river where we could wash the parts that needed it, our noses had begun to realise how long ago our last showers had been. A most luxurious wild site, Peter had not only found an old chair but there was an *en suite*. In the bushes was a complete pedestal with seat which I declined as my chair; so we used the other one he had found as a table for cooking supper. We thought our site completely private until, when we were having breakfast, three fishermen walked past and wished us "Bonjour".

Brignoles *boulangerie* provided even more tempting baguettes and I succumbed to the temptation to buy croissants for elevenses as well. What a good thing we needed to eat to keep up our energy levels, as we found French food irresistible, I became so enthusiastic about the *boulangeries* that Peter threatened to ban me. Brignoles seemed very much alive for a Sunday morning. We found an obliging bank 'hole-in-the-wall', which delivered just enough cash to get us through our last few days in France. There seemed to be plenty of shops open and plenty of cheerful people about, but thankfully little traffic and that devoid of lorries. More than anywhere else in France, there were people sitting outside cafés drinking coffee and taking a leisurely breakfast. In this town the habit was much in evidence, so although it was a busy place it felt very comfortable.

After forty-five kilometres we stopped to eat our croissants with our *jus* near Audeban. The countryside was becoming more hilly but not enough to impede progress. We found another of the picnic places with tables and benches, which makes life a little more civilised and added a sense of holiday to our, at times, gruelling expedition. We had intended to have lunch before Frejus, but found ourselves in the town almost before we realised it. This was when we made the mistake of the day. We did not do our provisioning before lunch when the shops were still open, and despite the fact that it looked like a holiday town, they did not open again that day. We had found a lovely park for lunch overlooking the Roman ruins of (we thought) an aqueduct. This was in addition to the ruins we had seen of a small colosseum (if that is not a contradiction in terms) on the way into the town. This area seemed rich in Roman remains; when we had been here before we had been taken to see a number of the more famous ones, including the magnificent Pont du Garde.

So, with dwindling stocks of food and drink, we set off to find a site, preferably a well equipped one with a shop! Coming up a hill out of the town, we saw and followed a sign which led us down a lane for two or three kilometres, until we arrived at a youth hostel site. Several tents but not a soul in sight. The notices on the office, when (very) roughly translated, indicated that campers should be members of a youth hostel association, which neither of us are. We retraced our pedals and getting hotter by the minute, returned to the road to carry on. Fortunately it was still early so we were not dispirited and soon found another campsite sign, this time to Camp Europa, which sounded a little more promising. We were greeted by an American obviously struggling with his French so I relented and told him we were English. Very relieved he explained he was trying to ask if we had booked as they were completely full! I told him that as we were on bicycles it was not practical to book ahead and pleaded with him to find us a little space – we would not take up nearly as much as those who come by car. He found us a tiny corner beside the ablutions and we pitched, very relieved to have found somewhere we could have a shower at last, the Camargue site seemed a long time ago.

This, our penultimate day in France, had been one of easy cycling though it was quite hot; the following day was to be another contrast. There was a form of a shop on the site but we could only buy a strange selection of items for our supper. The American did not know if there was a nearby shop as he was always too busy at the site. We bought, at horrendous prices, frankfurters, eggs at two francs each and a half litre of wine for twenty francs. It was only when our after-supper walk took us out of the site that we found a shop where we were able to stock up for the following day at more sensible prices. We tried our phonecard again and we did get through briefly, but were cut off twice. It was as well we were in the habit of turning in early as our restful night was cut short by the early risers going to and from the washrooms; it seemed the French campers started their days much earlier than the Spanish. These were a particularly jolly crowd all wishing each other "Bonjour" at the tops of their cheerful voices so we decided to join in. Even the pigeons here were noisy in their greetings! It was a relief that the site was not an expensive one – fifty francs for the night, which helped to make up for the exorbitant cost of our supper. On leaving the site, our first stop was the easily found bakery to treat the senses once more.

What a wonderful route over the mountain leaving Provence – though it was with some regret that we said farewell to this most beautiful region on the last morning of May. From Frejus to Cannes by the non-coastal route is much to be recommended. The climb, though long is gradual, the highest point being just below the peak marked six hundred and ten metres. We climbed for about eight kilometres through green woodland, mainly cork oak and broom, underlaid with wild flowers and definitely thought that the best way to enjoy it is by bike. Shortly after commencing the descent, we were delighted to come across a drinking fountain kindly provided by Madame Abreyette of New England in 1904. A refreshing drink, a chance to top up our water bottles and a good splash of faces and hands was much appreciated before the rest of the cooling descent to Cannes. A few kilometres short of the town, we stopped at a photogenic vista by the entrance to Les Escallions, a very exclusive-looking country club with stunning views.

Once into Cannes, everything changed. We had left the glorious rural landscape and were back in traffic, dust and bustle and to cap it all, I picked up a half inch No. 6 posidrive screw in my rear tyre. The best of the day was over. It would be nice to say the rest of the day is best forgotten but that would be cheating. Cannes was very hard work to get through. We had been away from busy towns for some time and had so enjoyed the absence of stress, but in Cannes we were back in the thick of it. We passed a millionaire's playground, a yacht harbour full of the most expensive looking boats, all idle and looking out in anticipation at the clear blue waters of the Mediterranean. We slogged along the road to Nice where we found, to our relief, a park for lunch and a bit of a rest from the traffic. It was a shaded circular area, benches set around a cooling fountain where we sat under the trees. Whilst having our lunch, the entertainment was from a pair of tramps, one of whom was going round begging cigarettes from the people in the park and giving them to the other man. I remember the other man was dressed in a loud yellow/brown checked suit, almost clown-like. All the time we were eating and drinking we thought it strange that we were the only ones not to be pestered. Perhaps our scruffy appearance made us look like tramps also, although he did not come and offer us a cigarette.

It was another stressful afternoon. We had been looking forward to seeing Monaco but when we finally reached it we were just too tired to appreciate it. We took the Basse Corniche road along the coast following the signs to Monte Carlo and dodging fast cars. It had been difficult to get onto the road; coming out of Nice we had encountered one of the 'forbidden zones', those parts of direct routes that suddenly confronted us with "No bicycles" signs. We had managed to divert to alternative roads; we knew that if we kept the sea on our right we would be going in basically the right direction, hoping to meet up with the correct road later on. It sounds like hit-and-miss navigation, but with our lack of a detailed map for the area and the frustrations of having to divert, it was not easy.

As the afternoon wore on, I was becoming anxious at the lack of signs for any campsites. There had been none between Cannes and Roquebrune-Cap Martin. Could it be that this stretch of the Riviera only offered hotel accommodation? That made us feel very out of place. As we rode into Monte Carlo we were dehydrating, we were thankful that we were aware of the dangers of this and had been keeping up our daily salt intake. We said we would stop at the next bar for a beer but impossible though it is to believe, we saw only one, and that on the opposite side of the road which was too busy to cross. Monte Carlo was obviously preparing for the Grand Prix, as there were stands being constructed along the road and crash barriers lined the harbour – it all looked very exciting. We did not know when the racing was to be, we just hoped to be through before any started. We cannot say we enjoyed Monaco, the late afternoon heat and exhaustion were getting the better of me. I felt very near to collapse, so for half an hour we sat on a low wall trying to rehydrate with our water bottles, feeling the situation was getting desperate. Trying to distract me, Peter told me to look at a passing Mercedes which we are sure was driven by Prince Rainier, looking very casual and relaxed, far from how we felt. We were still in too great a volume of traffic for comfort but we noticed an English holiday coach pass us; we were to recognise it the following day, just over the Italian border.

We had thought that Monaco bordered with Italy, and that we had seen the last of France but we still had a final night to spend on French soil. Finally we found a campsite alongside a noisy hotel called La Toraca. Although we had pitched right outside the restaurant window, we did not care about the noise that was mostly coming from a loud television. We had cycled from breakfast to supper and found the only campsite on the Riviera, the beer was cold and it was enormous. I was finding that, however tired I became during the afternoon, after a half-hour or so of complete relaxation, (preferably following a long cold beer) I was able to recover and enjoy a restful evening. We supped simply but gratefully and then had a short walk to look over to the Italian coastline – we had almost reached the border. In fact we feared we might have to cross over in our search for a campsite, there was certainly nowhere to camp wild since before Cannes. It was a day all the wrong way round, the lovely rural part at the beginning of the day, followed by the stressful, endless sprawl. We had clocked up a total of ninety-five kilometres, much of which would have been easier by car though we were not regretting our bicycles. The puncture that morning had been our first since the Camargue and we had had no mechanical problems. Our site at La Toraca was comfortable enough, and after the restaurant closed and the television was turned off, quieter than Europa. We realised that we had begun to find the heat more tiring and our water consumption was increasing during our days in the saddle. We might have to change our routine before long.

During our ten day stay in France, we had ridden 725 kilometres, had spent six nights on sites and three wild. Our cost of living had been an average of £10.50 each per day at exchange rate of 7.8 francs to the pound. We had really enjoyed this part of France; except for the final stretch which we do not recommend to cyclists, the remainder was wonderful. Some of the cycling had been hard work but was all worthwhile.

Chapter 12   Italy and Route Changes

A new month and a new country; we entered Italy on the first of June exactly seven kilometres after starting the day's cycling, and for the first few minutes viewed the country from within a couple of tunnels, divided by colourful bougainvillaea. Many years ago, whilst on holiday in France, I had been driven to Menton and just crossed the border so that we could say we had been to Italy. This time we were doing it for real, changing money at the border and seeing signs in another and unfamiliar language. It was time to change the Berlitz books again. Ventimiglia, our first town, which we reached at the end of the tunnels, gave us some idea of what to expect in Italian towns. It was a long town and full of traffic lights, but these did not prevent the traffic appearing to come at us from all directions so we felt we had to be even more alert. I also noticed there seemed to be public clocks everywhere; did this indicate that the Italians were very time-conscious, as the drivers always seemed to be in a hurry? We also noticed one of our most sought after signs, one for a campsite, but since we had just breakfasted, it was too early in the day.

Our map showed us that the S1, the Via Aurelia, was our road. It would eventually take us all the way to Rome, we just had to find it and stick to it.

Finding the Via Aurelia was easy, staying with it even easier, as it took us four days before we could escape from it, and we even had difficulties with that. The road from Ventimiglia led us along the Ligurian coast, an area of breathtaking scenery, straight out of a travel brochure with hillsides dropping dramatically into a sea the colour of sapphires. The road followed the coastline faithfully, up and down with steep cliffs to one side and a sheer drop to the sea on the other. The trouble with the Via Aurelia was its drama; the road was enclosed on both sides, which made it impossible to find anywhere to leave it even for a lunch break. The only roads off it were in the towns and these were few and far between. We did manage to find a tiny space between the barrier and cliffs for our lunch – it was tiny and not very inviting for a siesta so we had to carry on.

At Ventimiglia we had drawn a quarter of a million lire each and together we felt like half a millionaire, so it seemed appropriate to stop at Imperia to find a campsite. We had only travelled fifty kilometres that day but after the trauma of the previous one, (our final day in France), we felt that a short day was called for. Our campsite, opposite the free beach, was called De Wijnstock, sounding far more Dutch than Italian, though I was sure the proprietor was German. A pleasant and shady site, which had some already erected washing lines for me to do some much needed laundry. We had often camped within sound of noisy dogs, but at this site we were next to some of those frogs with unbelievably loud voices. The sound was similar to that on our last wild night in Portugal but the volume far greater. Our site was conveniently close to a large supermarket where we purchased *weetabix*, a two litre bottle of wine (for just over the equivalent of one pound) as well as tuna and fruit. We also bought more thick black thread to repair panniers and a pack of three brightly coloured T-shirts to replace those no-longer-white ones which we finally discarded.

Our first impressions of Italian roads were that they were very busy and the drivers all seemed to be in a tearing hurry. In the towns they all seemed to want to beat the traffic lights. The road we had been on so far was sadly littered which detracted a little from the beauty of the surroundings. The currency was also going to take some getting used to. Our first site had cost 18,000 lire which, when compared to fifty francs for the previous night, was most confusing, but was in fact very close when converted to sterling. As we were into June and it was usually very hot in the early afternoons, we would try to make early starts and aim to finish cycling about lunchtime. This plan was thwarted the next morning as we were unable to rouse the site owner to pay up and leave as early as we wanted to. It had an advantage though, as while we were waiting for him, I noticed I had left my towel on the borrowed washing line.

As we rode through Imperia we sensed it was a town of faded elegance, some impressive architecture but with shabby paintwork. In this part of Italy we saw some impressive wall paintwork, 'architectural' features painted onto flat walls and in Imperia it was mostly in need of repainting. I found it interesting how different countries had their individual styles such as the lovely tiled walls we had seen in Portugal.

We felt somewhat stifled by the Via Aurelia that day, as there was one tourist town after another and once again no way off the road. All the towns had beaches but the whole shore line was fenced off with fierce-looking high fences, entry was obviously by way of a fee. The day was rather overcast, which made for more comfortable cycling, but unfortunately the haze made the views a little less distinct. Our aim on this second day was to reach Savona, about fifty kilometres from Genova, thus giving us a late morning ride through the city. On the way to Savona we passed through tunnels which shortened the climbs just a bit but nonetheless we had some steep ones. Between every town was a steep headland or cliff to be won, but it was a lovely feeling to swoop down the far sides towards the towns. The coastal outcrops were partially shaded by pine trees and mostly clothed in golden broom flowers which smelled wonderful. On many of the hilltops were towers; one ruined castle was perched so precariously above the road that we were relieved to get past it. We were most amused by the 'Mini-H.G.V.s', the three-wheeler goods vehicles powered by moped engines, especially when we were able to overtake them. This road gave us such mixed feelings, those of being trapped and of being invigorated.

Approaching Savona we passed the seventy target for the day and were faced with three campsites, of which we chose Victoria, as it had a regal sound. It was right on the beach and had awnings under which to pitch. We managed to get our tent up just before the post-midday thunderstorm. We watched the grey clouds building up whilst we ate our lunch, before making a hasty retreat inside for the short duration of the refreshing rain. From the beach we could see that Savona was a fair-sized port and industrial town and the camp was between that and the residential area. Before tea we had a saunter out to buy food; how we wished we had brought our bikes as it was much farther than we had anticipated. Italian supermarkets seemed to be the first ones that did not press quantities of plastic carrier bags on us; although we had been finding them useful, we had to throw so many away. Not realising this, we had failed to bring any with us and we found that there was a charge for them, a good thing too. As we could not find the same cheap wine as the previous day, we bought some in boxes which proved to be so awful that for the first time we did not finish! We thought Camp Victoria an expensive site, 26,000 lire or £13, but the owner's wife had brought us a table and chairs, and of course it was on the beach which probably added to the cost, though it was far too cold for swimming.

Only fifty kilometres from Genova the following morning and the day was to have quite a bearing on the rest of the expedition. When visiting the city of Barcelona one of our aims had been to find a tourist or ferry office which could give us information about services from Genova which we could use on the way back. We had seen the ferry route marked on our maps, so we knew we could use them. We had not succeeded in Barcelona, but knowing that Genova was on the way, we had not been concerned. On Thursday 3rd June, the start of our eleventh week, we entered Genova with the intention of finding out about ferries from the other end.

Just before the city, in a small town, we were overtaken by a convoy of police cars and it was not until a few kilometres further on we realised what it was all about. They had set up a roadblock where policemen armed with machine guns were stopping and searching all the cars travelling into Genova. We slowed down but were waved on, so it was not us they were after. Genova was not a pleasant experience and it served only to reconfirm our many-times-learned lesson that cycles and cities are best kept apart. Lugo, Oporto, Sevilla and Barcelona had all put us off and Genova was just the icing on the cake. The first part of the city was quite respectable and took us along the promenade. it was always easy entering a town when all the signs were for the city centre, but when you reached the centre and were trying to find the signs for the next town along, it was always quite a different matter. Since we had added the complication of wishing to enquire about ferries we had to find the port. Heading for the water, we rode through the ugliest part of the town where the road ran level with (and sometimes shared) railway tracks. Past tall buildings which accentuated the noise of the unrelenting traffic, we finally found the port gates. We could see no ferry offices but Peter asked the port policeman who was able to tell us (in a good mixture of languages and gesticulations) that the ferries to Barcelona were no more ... our maps were out of date!

We were stunned. Ever since leaving England we had expected to use this ferry on the return journey, but now it seemed a radical change would be needed. However, first we had to find our way out of Genova. Our disappointment added to the stress, so it was with difficulty that we found the sign to La Spezia, which took us onto a stretch of elevated roadway that we doubted was for bicycles. We had not actually seen any prohibition signs; maybe it was that the road seemed too good for the likes of us or was it the shaking heads and wagging fingers of the passing motorists? At least we were on the Via Aurelia again, so we must be on the right road; the only place we could find for our lunch break was a narrow concreted lay-by.

The hills during the afternoon became longer and steeper but we were so thankful to be out of the city, with an ever-growing resolve to stick to rural roads with no exceptions. The map had shown the peninsula Santa Margherita as being a likely spot to look for a site, but as we passed it (no site signs) all we saw was a pinnacle in the clouds. The scenery was improving greatly, the first real countryside since just after Frejus and we were optimistic of somewhere really lovely for the night. We found it. After a marvellous downhill run to Rapallo, the first sign we came to was for Camp Miraflores and it was perfect. A pretty grassed site of fairly private terraces, each with its own concrete table and benches. The only disadvantage was that the motorway passed rather close above us which meant some noise. The concrete table was spread with maps and some serious planning ensued. So serious that we had to interrupt it for a shopping trip and then shelter in the tent for half an hour to wait for the daily thunderstorm to pass. Out maps again, this time with mugfuls of wine to aid the brain cells. If 'no more cities' was to be the rule, then it was good-bye to the prospect of Rome and Naples; we had really wanted to see Rome and Pompei but our sanity and comfort were paramount. The days had become hot and promised to get more so, which added to the stress we were feeling when in traffic, so the prospect of cycling the length of Italy had lost its attraction. The intention had been to ride all the way to Brindisi at the heel of Italy and catch the ferry to Igouinenitsa (on the Greek mainland near Corfu). Now it was time to look for an alternative, particularly since we were not going to be able to get a ferry back to Barcelona. The map also showed us that Bari and Ancona were ferry ports, Ancona being the more northerly and nearer. It also showed that Livorno (on the west coast) sent ferries to Corsica with onward ferries to Marseilles, but could we trust the map?

It seemed there were several possibilities, mostly dependent on whether the map information was correct or not. Having definitely decided against Rome and therefore Southern Italy, which would have included Pompei and Brindisi, we were beginning to look towards Ancona as a possible port of departure, though we did not make a firm decision until we obtained the timetables at Pisa. We were currently between the mountains and the sea, a narrow strip that we must keep to as far as Tuscany, so we still needed to stick to the Via Aurelia. The only way to escape from her was by the mountain passes due north and we did not want to add to our mountain climbing, besides there were still some places to visit on this side of the Appenines. If we stuck to the planned route for a little longer we would pass close to Pisa, so we made that our next landmark; maybe we could have a weekend there.

Our evening at Miraflores was most remarkable for the theatrical entertainment to which we were treated after dusk. I had just returned from my last visit of the day and crawled into my sleeping bag, and Peter was cleaning his teeth close to the tent when he saw a strange flashing light which he took to be a reflection. It was quickly repeated so he wondered about phosphorescence, a distant flashing light or what? Excitedly he called to me as he realised it was similar in intensity to the glow-worm rarely seen at home. We both stood transfixed at this phenomenon, neither of us had ever seen fireflies before. More and more of them appeared until we were in the midst of an aerial ballet of flashing 'fairy lights', some as close as an inch or so from our faces, others filling the hedgerows and all across the campsite. So brightly they shone, that once back in our sleeping bags we could still follow their lights through the tent fabric as they passed on their busy way. We were to be treated to two more evenings of these displays, once in the mountains high above the west coast and again beside the river whose valley led us to Ancona.

The area between Rapallo and La Spezia was probably the most picturesque of Liguria, but we worked hard to enjoy it. We left the coast the following afternoon to cross inland of Cinque Terre as Aurelia climbed up to the Passo de Branco beyond Deiva Marina. There did not appear to be a coastal road through this part, only side roads that did not join up, branching off to each settlement. We were approaching the Alpi Apouane mountains where they come close to the sea beyond La Spezia, there were white tops to them even though it was June. We took our lunch break at Passo de Branco (613 metres) which had been thoughtfully equipped with a bar and we felt we had earned this beer. We settled down for our bread and cheese just beyond the pass with the most photogenic scenery and felt really relaxed – 'This is what it is all about'. Whilst we munched, a large young Austrian mountain biker rode up and stopped for a chat. We felt somewhat humbled, as all the Europeans we met conversed with us in English and all we were able to come up with were our few short phrases from our books for shopping. He told us he was camping with his family at Deiva Marina and cycled up to the pass every day just for fun; we commented on his greater number of gears and lack of luggage, at which he laughed and agreed it did make his riding much easier. As he left we concentrated on building up our energy reserves for the rest of the day. It had been a tiring climb up and we hoped the rest would all be downhill.

For the most part it was, cooling downhill runs are most enjoyable but we realised we would not reach La Spezia that day. Would we be able to camp wild? We had not yet done so in Italy and we did not see level ground anywhere. This road over the mountains was affording far more open countryside, it had taken four days to reach and it was wonderful. Although the road was still steep we were no longer hemmed in by barriers with steep drops to the side, and there was plenty of vegetation. The mountains were green and not a bit barren. The big surprise of the day was when, at about 4.30pm, without warning, there was a campsite. It was Branchetta Villa and seemed to be in the middle of nowhere. No village, no shops, how we thanked our foresight in bringing an emergency meal, even though it was only rice with packet soup followed by bread and fruit. Although the motorway had been noisy at Rapallo, we blessed it, as it had meant an empty road for us, we had only seen one lorry, and that while we were having our lunch off the road. I am sure that in previous years, all vehicles would have travelled the Aurelia and that would not have been fun. All we had seen of the motorway had been in the distance, usually vertically below us as it entered or emerged from tunnels, or occasionally high above us on stilts.

We were certainly changing our opinion of Italy – we had expected it to be rather bare, mountainous and to look somewhat burned. We had not visualised such lush greenery, as for the second consecutive night we were camping on grass. We had come through some incredibly beautiful countryside and were treated to another firefly display. We had also had a day of flowers, many familiar, such as briar roses and chestnut trees in flower, but also some white orchids and brilliant pink sweet peas all growing wild beside the road.

The next day it was back to the coast and to a holiday-maker's haven. We set off good and early, having been surprised to be awakened by a church bell. As it happened, there was a village just over the hill from the site that we did not see until the morning. It was all downhill to La Spezia with very little pedalling, a run of nearly forty kilometres. Just before the town were tremendous hairpin bends which we negotiated with great caution, remembering the blowout that Peter's brakes had caused in Spain. We saw an Italian teenager chugging his way up on a scooter, talking away ten to the dozen on a mobile phone. The bends reminded me of mountain biking in Corfu, where we attempted to ride up Mount Pantekrator but ended up instead in a deserted mountain village.

In La Spezia we found the sign for Pisa, although the sign also stated ninety (kilometres to go), it was very cheering to see our next target in writing. La Spezia was a busy tourist town and built around an inlet. We had come over the area named Cinque Terre, could this be translated as Five Lands or even Five Mountains? We felt as if we had climbed more than five. The downhill runs had been so good and we felt our general level of fitness must be at its best during this stage of the journey, as walking up the mountains did not seem to bother us greatly. They obviously slowed us down but we did not mind. Although we did get very tired at times, we found our energy returned fairly quickly. The mountainous part when combined with clement weather, made for far more interesting travel than the flatter parts of Italy.

After La Spezia we were onto more level ground, a flat and narrow plain between the mountains and the sea. Almost all the way to Pisa, the Alpi Apouane rose to our left, but as we entered Tuscany the plain widened. From La Spezia, once we found the coastal road, there was a continuous sprawl of holiday towns most being called Marina Di...(named after the nearest town a few miles inland). For lunch we stopped in a park, near to which we saw a strange structure looking like a shopping mall. This was pleasing to us as we needed some food; however, on closer inspection, it proved to be a fee-paying beach with an impressive entrance. By mid-afternoon we realised we had entered Marina Di Carrera, having done sixty kilometres, and there we found signs for twenty campsites. The first two we rejected, one for its situation, too close to the noisy road, the second for its price. The third looked a bit more scruffy and Peter went in and negotiated a good price, 12,000 lire. It always amused me that the £ sign was used to denote lire, so it seemed we were paying a fortune for even the most basic items. We had also been impressed that so many of the site operators spoke, or at least attempted to speak, English, thus putting us in our place again.

At Marina Di Carrera we found a public weighing machine and having collected the correct change we used it. Peter weighed in at 68.5 kilos and I at 54.5; converting this to imperial meant we had each lost over a stone and we were at the stage of putting weight back on thanks to the *weetabix*. It would have been interesting to find out what we had been at our lowest point, possibly another half a stone less.

From the prom we saw another of those truly wonderful sunsets, the best since Provence. The site was rather scruffy, it had the air of a shanty town as amongst the static caravans were some home-made chalets or shacks, but it was a friendly place if a bit noisy. The noise mostly came from one of the chalets near us which was occupied by a group of youngsters enjoying a Saturday night and obviously not in need of sleep as we were. Consequently we started the next day later than we hoped to, we were quite glad to leave the sea and enter the peaceful countryside of Tuscany. We had to spend more time with Aurelia although we kept thinking we had seen the last of her. To think, if we had kept to our original plan to go to Rome, we would have been in her company for another few weeks! However, as she led us into Tuscany she had become more bicycle-friendly – we felt we had formed quite a relationship.

The interesting part of this Sunday morning was through Petro Santi, a town of marble and alabaster. All along the road for some kilometres were stacks of marble slabs, all sizes and colours, many of which were beautifully polished to show off colour and grain. We heard the whine of a saw at work, so there was overtime for the employees. In places, we saw alabaster fashioned into statues and ornaments and we passed sales centres, one after the other beside the road which also displayed large colourful pottery.

Beyond Viareggio the countryside really opened out, the mountains had receded to the north and the more gently rolling hills of Tuscany were about us, with much evidence of agriculture. We stopped for a break about twenty kilometres short of Pisa as we had found a couple of trees for shade, there was less and less of this and the heat was increasing. Pisa was reached far sooner than expected, our first glimpse being through some sparse trees over fields straight to the leaning tower and the buildings alongside. It was an amazing sight; there it was, the tower of which one hears from an early age and we were looking at it. We had expected it to be hemmed in by high buildings but it was in plain sight.

With a wonderful feeling of achievement we rode into the first site we came to, 'La Torrente Pendente' (the leaning tower) with the unspoken agreement we would not move again for a couple of nights. Although we had only ridden fifty kilometres that day we had not had a day off since 27th May, ten days ago and we had ridden seven hundred and fifty kilometres since then! This site at Pisa was an extensive grassed one with hedges and more trees than we had seen in most of the Tuscan countryside. We picked a spot by the hedge to pitch and acquired a table and chairs which lay around for the campers to use. Civilisation again, we could set out our food above ground level. This was to be one of the sites where we felt most relaxed and at home. Later that afternoon we met an English couple, a retired geology professor and his geographer wife, Professor and Mrs Cope, who proved to have an extensive knowledge of the area. They told us they had been coming to Italy for many years, always staying in Pisa for a few days as they had friends nearby.

During the evening our little company was joined by a old VW camper van with GB plates, containing a young couple. Later Mrs Cope told Peter that she had spoken to them and the girl was a Midlander, so he resolved to strike up a conversation next time he saw them. When he asked the girl whereabouts she came from, she said "Oh, you wouldn't know it" so he said, "Try me". When she replied "Whiteheath", Peter answered, "Well fancy that, I used to live in Throne Road." (a road leading off Whiteheath) – that really did make the world seem smaller. They were able to spend a while reminiscing about their home town.

Pisa came up to expectations and more. We were so fascinated by actually seeing the leaning tower that we just could not keep away. The immediate area was fenced off but there was a large grassed area where people of all nations assembled to gaze and wonder as we did. Though we had camped only a kilometre away, we used our bicycles to ride in and it was a wise choice. Pisa was full of cycles. It appeared to be quite in order to ride them all over the town, any where, any how and any direction. In fact they seemed to be going both ways along one way streets and on either side. The atmosphere was so relaxed and this was to be the most 'cycle friendly' town we found during the whole of our trip. As we had arrived on a Sunday afternoon, most of the town was closed up except for the square around the tower, where the most amazing prices were being asked for postcards and souvenirs; one poor woman was so staggered at being asked a four-figure amount for a postcard she fell backwards into Peter who kindly set her on her feet again. We were interested to see a large contingent from a cycling club all having their photos taken, we even saw another pair of heavily loaded touring bikes parked near ours which had by this time been stripped. We did relent and buy a couple of ice creams which cost us £1 each but waited until we returned to the site to buy postcards. From one of these we learned all about the tower; begun in 1174 by Bonanno Pisanon, completed ninety-nine years later by Giovanni de Simone, it is 186 feet high, fifty feet in diameter, has eight floors and 294 steps, but however did they weigh it to discover it has a weight of 14.732 tons? There are also seven bells and the oldest goes by the name of Pasquereccia.

We spent the first evening at Pisa chatting to our new English friends. This was one of the nicest aspects of campsites abroad, that we could go round looking for GB plates and meet up with some most interesting people. Professor Cope and his wife were fascinating conversationalists as they had visited the area so many times and were able to advise on possible future routes across the country. Pisa was their halfway point – the following morning she was having a sort out, which meant changing from winter things to summer before proceeding to the south of the country for a month or so. He was a gentleman of mature years (eightyish) who had driven all across the Alps towing a large caravan as apparently he does every year – we were very impressed.

We spent our second day at Pisa re-provisioning and searching for a travel agent to obtain ferry information. Once in possession of the timetables for the Livorno to Bastia crossings and onwards to Marseilles, we knew we had another viable alternative way home, we could cross through France and go south of the Pyrenees to Santander. Being attracted by the thought of ferries, we decided definitely to go to Ancona which would give us the chance to visit Assisi en route, a town which we realised we very much wanted to see.

Having bought a postcard of the floodlit tower, we ventured forth after dusk but were a bit disappointed to see it was not lit up, no doubt that was for special occasions only. We had lost count of the times we had been to look at the tower, so fascinated were we by it. We had really seen one of the official wonders of the world to add to those on our own list.

Leaving Pisa on the 8th of June, we felt yet another stage completed. We would soon be leaving the west side of Italy to go inland and could expect to approach the Apennines; to reach the other side of the country we would have to cross Italy's backbone and we wondered how knobbly it would be. Most of the numbers on the map referred to distances or road identification, only a few marked the heights of mountains and many of these were over 1000 metres.

The big question that morning was – how far would we have to ride before we escaped Aurelia's clutches? We had not left her at Pisa, we could not go directly to Florence as it was motorway, so we had to find the little white road running alongside. Initially this meant taking the road for Livorno although that was well south of where we wanted to go. After passing an extensive military camp (a good three kilometres long) with lovely pine woods opposite, we found the S67, a flat, narrow, winding country lane passing farms and fields which we had all to ourselves. We were so glad we could not use the motorway, for once it would not have been as direct as our little road. Our compass confirmed that we were travelling in the right direction so we had all the advantages. We kept the motorway close by, mainly elevated but at one point we wondered why it was not covered by rushing traffic. As we got closer we could see it was still under construction although our map had not given us that detail, so we were thankful we had found the S67.

At Pontedera we replaced the scissors I had broken a couple of days previously when cutting up my discarded T-shirt to make bike cleaning rags. Not that it had needed much cutting up but our plastic handled scissors were not strong enough for my well developed hand-muscles! The new scissors were christened that evening to give me a much needed haircut. We camped for the night in the corner of a cornfield about five kilometres from Certaldo as we had no known sites to aim for. The Copes, with their book of Italian campsites, assured us we would have to ride to San Gimigniano to find one and that was impossible, about one hundred kilometres from Pisa. We pitched at the bottom of a tiny valley, which should have had a stream but did not. It was our first wild camp in Italy so we were a little anxious. We had pitched against a camouflaging hedge when the after-tea harvesters suddenly arrived to cut corn for an hour. They were using a machine that looked like a large lawn mower and it must have been hard work. We felt sure that would ask us our business so we prepared some hopefully suitable phrases of request from our Italian book, but they were not needed. After their hour of work they went on their way. They had been at the far end of the field and not seemed bothered by our presence. We were very glad to be able to stay, as it was a very steep push to get out of the field and we would not have known where else to go.

We passed an otherwise peaceful evening amongst the Tuscany farmland. It had been a day of gentle hills as the higher ones thankfully had kept their distance. We had passed vines, fields of grain, alfalfa and even sunflowers. At Castelfiorino, where we had to wait for the shops to open, we sat in a park shaded by magnolia, oleander and plane trees. I sat with the bikes while Peter went off buying extra bottles of water and, having taken pity on the bike-guard, some cans of beer, which arrived lovely and cold.

For once, we did leave some evidence after our wild camp. I wonder what the locals might have made of a square of flattened grass and a pile of human hair by the corner of their corn field. Feeling somewhat light-headed, we left still heading inland towards Siena. Our first town was Poggibonsi where we found a supermarket and the way to another deserted road, this time the S2. We had entered Italy on the S1 which had become the Via Aurelia; this S2 was the Via Fassia, which took us to Siena and would have taken us to Rome also, had we let it.

Although it would have been pleasant to stop in Siena and look for art galleries, we had arrived at midday, not a good time for sight-seeing and too early to take advantage of the campsite sign we saw as we rode in. The road to Perugia was easy to find and it was another excellent cycling road, level, well surfaced and with lovely scenery. This turned out to be one of our hottest days and we had used up much of the previous day's purchased water. We still had enough for the day's riding but consumption had increased considerably. We covered the twenty kilometres from Siena to Rappalano Terme before lunch, but towards the latter town I was wilting uncomfortably and feeling very weak. Just outside the town we found a stream to splash over our heads, and have a short rest before going in search of a bar for long cold beers. Unfortunately, as it was early afternoon, all the shops were shut, but after the beer we felt much better, so we rode off a short distance where we found a grassy bank with a large shady tree to spend the afternoon relaxing and replacing Peter's broken spoke (the first spoke break we had experienced).

After four o'clock, when we hoped the shops would reopen, we sauntered back into Rappalano to buy some supper. We still did not know where we would spend the night but this was hospitable-looking countryside – such a contrast to the previous week. After visiting every food shop we could find, Peter asked someone, who told him that it was Wednesday early-closing in Rappalano. This time we had no emergency meal as we had not replaced the one consumed only a few days before. Our larder pannier had only a little bread and cheese left, so we might have to eat at the bar. As luck would have it we saw a grocer who was just taking in a delivery and kindly let us buy some food and wine. Yet again we were quite convinced we were being looked after, these things seemed to happen to help us.

Cycling just a short distance from the town we found the loveliest wild site Italy could have provided – 'Broom Corner'; just off a side road, it was the corner of a field amongst green and golden broom bushes. We had reached the end of our eleventh week of cycling, a week when we had covered almost four hundred and twenty kilometres (even though we had spent two nights at Pisa) and had clocked a total of almost 5000 kilometres. We had definitely decided to go to Ancona to look for a ferry to Greece, the heat of that day and my near-collapse experience before lunch had made us discount the possibility of trying to return across Italy in late July – we would look for a different route home. When we had been in Corfu a few years previously we had heard of an overland coach from there to London which might be a possibility, or might we even fly back? There were various ideas floating around our heads, whatever way we did travel we wanted to bring our faithful machines with us, to dump them the far side of Europe would have been so ungrateful.

We even thought we might have a shower just as dusk fell, surrounded by grey clouds, we were sure we heard a few drops of rain on the tent. Hoping it would be the start of something useful, we stripped off and crawled outside only to spend a few minutes dancing about stark naked to no avail. The shower had been just the few spots of rain we had heard. Feeling a bit stupid we scrambled back into the tent laughing our heads off, thank heavens for the privacy.

We awakened at 6.30am to one of the most beautiful mornings. Despite the lack of rain it was all fresh, bright and quite cool. I re-stitched a pannier strap before we set out for a good easy ride to Perugia. Some of the road signs had us quite baffled, some that stated a town name and distance actually meant that the junction for that town would be at that distance and not the town itself. That explained why towns that I thought were some distance away from our road seemed as if they should be straight ahead. Just after crossing the motorway, our road became a dual carriageway which had us speeding down to the Lago Di Trasimeno (Lake Trasimeno, which is in the centre of Italy). We thought this road too good to be true but there had been no prohibition signs and anyway it was not a motorway. However after our elevenses break, we returned to the road and saw a set of unwelcoming signs. We had already ridden ten kilometres on it so cautiously we carried on, as if in blissful ignorance. After half an hour we were passed by a police-car which soon after stopped in a lay-by. Conscience came to the fore and we fully expected to be pulled over. Looking straight ahead of me I went past in the lead but as Peter drew level the policeman wagged a finger, looked questioningly at him but waved him past – what a relief. We had been behaving ourselves perfectly as usual, but the sight of a foreign policeman makes one a bit nervous, as not having enough of the language to explain that we could not find any other way would have been very tricky. Later we were told there had been a terrorist bomb in Florence and police were everywhere.

We spent a very pleasant afternoon and evening at a site on the shore of Lake Trasimeno. This was one occasion when we used a tourist information office to find a site and, in addition, were given some interesting literature about the area. Being centrally placed in Italy, the lake makes a wonderful holiday centre for touring this part of the country which is especially rich in art treasures. Whilst on the Riva Verde site, we met an English couple, Alex and Terry, who were here for just this purpose. They not only told us much about Assisi but gave us a larger-scale map so we could get there more easily. This lakeside site was conveniently placed so that we saw the sun setting over the water from our tent and had a view of two of the islands. One of them, the Isla Maggiore had sheltered St Francis for a period of his solitary prayer. The lakeside has medieval castles on its shores and we discovered it was the site of Hannibal's victory over the Romans in 217 BC. Had we not been so impatient to get on with the expedition, this would have been a perfect spot to have stayed for a few days though many of the places of interest were more suitable locations for drivers than for us. We kept telling ourselves that this expedition was one of exploration, finding places to which we would like to return on holidays in the future when we would make time to linger and really appreciate the countries. Whether we ever will do this is of course only conjecture, but one can always hope. We felt this would be a marvellous site on which to camp and see the treasures of Italy – however we would need motor transport so that, like our new friends, we could go and explore the museums and galleries. As it was we were heading for the next highlight of the trip – Assisi.

The map we had been given enabled us to pass Perugia taking the pleasanter and more direct route by narrower roads. Just half a day's journey to Assisi and one with only two hills that we had to push up and roads almost empty of vehicles. As we rode through Bastia we had our first sight of Assisi, nestling against Mount Subassio (424 metres). It was perched on its own little hill and the famous churches showed up distinctly. Just a few kilometres short of the town we found Camping International, a large open site only for tourers and tents, again grass and trees. It was time to award ourselves another 'weekend'.

What a town Assisi is! Another place of pilgrimage like Santiago but there the similarity ends. Built over the top of a hill, the views are exceptional and it is surmounted by the Rocca Maggiore, the ruins of a castle. The town itself is a mass of narrow little streets, some stepped and all at curious angles to each other. For our first visit we caught the 'site bus' (which turned out to be the receptionist's car) and walked back. We spent a wonderful afternoon walking the streets and absorbing the atmosphere. Basically the town is 12th century and appears mostly unchanged. The site office had given us a street map which made it easier to find the churches that we most wanted to see. The first and largest we went to was of course that of St Francis; as there was a service in progress, we stopped to listen and I was struck by the atmosphere of peace and prayer. We also visited those dedicated to St Clare and St Anthony. St Clare's was very austere, empty, and for me, lacking in feeling, but St Anthony's I found more comfortable. There was more decoration and a statue of St Anthony holding a child, both with very happy expressions on their faces. The streets were thronged with people of all colours and probably creeds, many of them monks or nuns, some of whom appeared to be guides. I felt there was an aura of calm over the town in contrast to bustling Santiago and to most of the other towns we had visited. We found a travel agent and obtained a timetable for the Ancona ferries which enabled us to confirm our plans. We could set out from Assisi with far more confidence.

For our full day there we used our bikes to travel about as the walk back from the town had been longer than we realised, about four kilometres and hot and tiring. In the morning we awoke at 5.30am to the sound of many bells, so many churches with different peals drowning the sound of the raindrops on our tent. We managed to go back to sleep for a while, before waking to watch a cloud dump its load over Mount Subassio. We decided to get the domestic business out of the way first, a trip to Bastia for shopping and to catch up on the laundry which I had not bothered with at Lake Trasimeno. That left the rest of the day free. Diverting a little, we went to look at the nearby village, St Maria del Angelo, dominated by a magnificent basilica church which was to be our favourite. It was undoubtedly the most beautiful we had seen, the frescoes were superb but most of all we liked the tiny original church in the centre of the building which is used as a chapel. As there was a wedding in progress, there was even more to enjoy – it was a very happy building. Outside in the square we could see the gilded statue of St Mary on the roof summit.

From Santa Maria, we cycled on into Assisi as we wanted to find our way to the top of the town and visit the fortress Rocca Maggiore. It was quite hard to find our way, as none of the streets go in a straight direction, but that made it all the more fun. We had to push through most of the town, as the streets were so steep and where they were not too steep there were too many people. Most of the streets are cobbled, which made for a bumpy ride down again. When we arrived at the fortress it was locked, but the views made the climb well worthwhile. Mount Subassio was the highest, but there were many other hills to see. We felt very elevated at the Rocca; it was interesting to look down on the jumble of rooftops and to see the tops of the churches below. Up here were sun and flowers and only a few other people. Assisi joined the list of places we were really glad we had been to.

Just to complete our weekend feeling, we treated ourselves to a pizza supper in the site restaurant. The choice was so large it took almost as long to work out the menu as to eat the meal. After dark we sat in the tent doorway watching a firework display we thought might have been staged to celebrate the wedding. Had we been prepared to stay longer, we could have seen more of the surrounding area, the Hermitage and the Abbey of San Behetto, both on the slopes of the mountain, but these would have to wait for another visit – we both felt we would like to come back some day.

On Sunday, June 13th, the bells of Santa Maria, deep and resonant, were the ones to start us moving! They were joined by all those of the many other churches within hearing so they really encouraged us. Another new gas cylinder to fit before breakfast meant one less to carry. Unfortunately I managed to leave Peter's sandals behind at this site, though we did not discover the loss until the evening, so I was in the doghouse till we reached Greece where we replaced them! On our way from the site, we stopped at Santa Maria to photograph the church although the morning was cloudy; at least we were in for a cool and comfortable start.

The S75 dual-carriageway gave us a long downhill run past Assisi and the mountain to Foligno. As we passed Spello, a town of similar architecture to Assisi, we watched the crowds of the faithful going into their large church. Most of the towns we passed that morning seemed to be clinging to their hills. In this part of Umbria, topography appears to dictate building and we saw very little habitation between the hills. As we turned northwards towards Nocera, we felt we must soon approach the Apennines, surely our climb over the backbone of Italy could not be delayed much longer. We had been incredibly lucky with the terrain since Pisa, the only really steep part had been just before the lake. Both Tuscany and Umbria had been so kind and green, not the barren rocky hillsides we had expected in the interior. The road heading north was the Via Flaminia, a road mentioned in Anne Musto's book as the most beautiful she had cycled in Italy. She describes the descent to Pesaro as being particularly scenic and invigorating but we did not go so far north, just as far as Nocera, where we turned east to climb over to Ancona.

Just before Nocera Peter had the first puncture in Italy. This forced a stop beside a level crossing, where we leaned up against the railway house and changed the tube to the delight of the assembled company. A group of old men who had gathered in the bar (which happened to be the additional occupation of the crossing keeper's cottage) came out to watch us. Whether they were impressed by the speed at which Peter changed the tube, or the sight of us heading for the mountains with such heavily loaded bikes, we shall never know. Probably we just provided a diversion for their Sunday morning chat. This was the first and only puncture in Italy.

After Nocera, we turned north-east onto the S361, the Septempadema, this was the 'Trans-Apennine' route taking us up to the Passo Cornetto (813 metres). This road must have been chosen for us; we had been very uncertain which road to take to reach the east coast as the map showed several which crossed the mountains. Red roads probably indicated better surfaces and slighter gradients. Our original first choice started off as the yellow S77 but it became dual-carriageway with the risk of prohibition, the S76 went rather too far north for us, but the S361, though only a yellow road, did seem to follow a river valley once over the top. This was the one we settled on, mainly because of the River Potenza; working on the theory that rivers flow downhill, it proved to be the ideal choice. It was almost completely empty and the actual climb not very long at all – we had passed the summit and were on the way down before lunch. Just before the top I had to go and spend a penny, where I was startled by a large snake which I had almost sat on – Peter was highly amused. At the summit was an unlit, curving tunnel which meant we had to turn on the dynamos and launch ourselves into the dark unknown. Thankfully this was the only time we found an unlit tunnel, it was a great relief that we did not have to share it with any other traffic. As we passed the summit, we clocked fifty-two kilometres, little did we realise how many more were to come that day! The source of the River Potenza was found quite quickly and we were very pleased, all downhill to the sea, or was it? The following thirty kilometres passed with hardly a turn of the pedals, we were really swooping down off the mountain. Once on the eastern side of it, the weather changed. Before lunch we met showers so we did not linger over our bread and cheese. It was so cold we actually had to put on our tracksuits for the rest of the descent. No more butterflies sunning themselves, as we had seen on the way up.

We had now left Umbria and were in Marche province, our final one in Italy. Coming down the valley, we passed through several small towns, Castelraimondo, Severino Marche and at Porcina we rode through some rough hewn limestone semi-tunnels. They were mostly open-sided, covered galleries and very light and white, rather like riding through a cave with windows in one side.

Once the river valley broadened and the land became agricultural again, we realised we should look for a wild site. There was no indication of official sites and we were still at least fifty kilometres from the sea, so the chance was more than remote. At four o'clock we passed the one hundred kilometre point and we were set to break the record. It took a further twenty to find somewhere to camp, a raised sandbank at the edge of the river near Villa Potenza, where the sign post told us it was only fifty-two to Ancona. We had not found any shops that afternoon but we had replaced our emergency rations, so we had a meal, though for the first time no wine, so after 5251 kilometres we finally opened the miniature of brandy we had been given by our neighbour before departure. Fortunately we had sufficient drinking water with us and plenty to wash in alongside.

Unknown to us this was our final night in Italy and we were treated to the most spectacular firefly display; the primadonnas all around us, as we sat by the tent, so close we could have held them in our hands and the chorus back as far as the hedge. We were still amazed by the dancing fairy lights – it was a sight so new to us. We were also astounded that in one day we had crossed the country's backbone and had completed one hundred and twenty kilometres of cycling, a record we would be content to let stand...or so we thought.

Some of the birds seemed to have been up all night singing and the rest joined in it about 5am accompanied by the sound of rain-drops. Perhaps we had reached the wetter side of the country, but why worry? Although we did not know it, this was to be our last day in Italy, we had been in the country exactly two weeks. We knew we should reach Ancona during the day but did not know how long we should have to wait for a ferry. We were sure we should find a campsite in or near the town.

With our rainproofs seeing the light of day for the first time since Barcelona, we set off to follow the signs for Ancona, the first one was within a few metres of regaining the road. By putting our trust in this, we made a mistake. It seemed logical to follow the sign but we should instead have stuck to the river Potenza, which had looked after us so well the previous day. Instead we turned north on the 'direct' road, the one that visited every little town on the way to Ancona, and every little town was built on its own little hill. After I had walked up at least five hills, Peter admitted he had 'messed with' my gears, so he had to make readjustments before I ceased to slow him down. After about half an hour the rain stopped and we found a shop, to our relief, as we were down to one meal's worth of cheese and half of cornflakes. In the village we also found a drinking fountain to refill our bottles.

It was a morning of ups and downs but we knew each one was taking us nearer to Ancona and the end of our time in Italy. We do not know whether we looked like natives but a woman motorist stopped Peter to ask if she was on the right road for Montecassio. To his amazement, he understood exactly what she was asking, and with a nod of his head, pointing his arm and a cheery "Si", each carried on in their respective correct directions. It had all happened so quickly and naturally, it was only afterwards he realised he had been asked a question and answered in Italian (admittedly only one word) without hesitation.

After Osimo (the last hill up which we had to push) the S361 ended and we joined the Via Adriatica. The Septempadema had been a kind road though we realised we should have left it at Villa Potenza and avoided all these little hills, but it had been such a good crossing of the mountains that we forgave it the terrain of the morning. The Via Adriatica is the main arterial road of the Adriatic coast before the motorway was built and is still a very busy road. As we joined it, we decided to stop for our break before running the risk of entering the expected urbanisation and possibly having nowhere to leave the road. Having seen a sign that told us we were within twenty kilometres of Ancona, we continued along the Adriatica with mounting excitement. What would we find at Ancona? Would we find a site first and then go looking for the ferry port? How long would we have to wait for the ferry to Greece? Would the booking procedure be straightforward? Were we in for a surprise?

At least the Via Adriatica was completely flat but that meant thundering lorries passing us all the while. Fortunately the distance signs were right and very quickly we were into the town. We rode in looking for campsite sign but saw none, so we headed for the port instead. Just before we reached it, I spotted a travel agent, so I went in to ask about campsites. I was told that the nearest one was along the coast about thirteen kilometres away but the port was just around the corner. So off we went to find out about the ferries first. At the port were numerous shipping line offices, but as we had previously obtained the timetables for Anek Lines, we headed for that office. The official asked when we wanted to go and when we replied "As soon as possible", he told us to go immediately to the dockside booking office, as there was one sailing that afternoon! An English-speaking clerk was happy to take our booking for the first available, the five o'clock sailing, boarding at three! The fare was £252,000 (lire – equivalent to £110 sterling) which was for two single tickets with the bicycles travelling free. We could hardly believe it was so easy to get a ferry booking. We had ridden into Ancona at noon and we were to board three hours later. In the remaining short time we had to buy food for the next thirty-six hours, have our lunch and prepare ourselves physically and mentally to complete one stage of the journey and to start the next. Having lunched on the quayside next to our ship, *The Kydon*, at exactly three o'clock we went into passport control. From there we wheeled our bikes onto the car deck, tethered them to the rail and took our front panniers and food to the passenger lounge. We could have opted for 'Porta Ponte' (deck only and grab a plastic chair if you can), but we treated our bones to aircraft-type seats for the twenty-four hour crossing.

Our stay in Italy suddenly completed, we calculated we had cycled 830 kilometres in fourteen days. We had spent ten nights on sites and had camped wild three times. Our cost of living averaged £13 each per day at exchange rate of 2,240 lire to the pound; our most expensive country to date.

Chapter 13 A Change of Pace

This really was a change of pace, in fact boarding the ferry marked a complete change in the whole expedition. We considered we had now completed the cycling in mainland Europe, at least for the outward leg. We decided that for the many places in Greece on our itinerary, we would hire a car. The heat of the last few days had convinced us that it would be a sensible move. We were also coming to the conclusion that neither of us really wanted to retrace our tyretracks back across Europe and we were by now almost looking forward to going home, it was mid-June and we had been away for twelve weeks and just beginning to think about the home comforts we had missed. We had proved to ourselves that survival without so much was not only possible but quite endurable, as long as we knew it would all be waiting back there for us.

Certainly the crossing of twenty-four hours gave us time for reflection. We had ridden 5,300 kilometres in just under twelve weeks and experienced a total change in our lives. We had spent all but five nights under canvas and in such a variety of weathers and places. The sights we had seen of Europe from the saddle could not be equalled by any other form of transport except possibly on foot, but the distances would then have been seriously curtailed. I think, above all, we felt a great sense of achievement and privilege that we had been able to do it. (When I looked back over my experiences of the past years, my stroke and my curious staccato recovery from it, it seems impossible that this could have been done.)

The Kydon was the smallest of the Anek Lines ferries on this route, it was fairly old, noisy and vibrating. When we saw it later from a distance, we realised it also had a marked list, but as it was flat calm on this crossing we had not noticed. We spent most of the evening on the deck reading, watching the Italian coastline disappearing and eating our sandwich supper. There were plenty of chairs and tables so we were in luxury. Had we been making the crossing in the height of the season, it would probably have been very crowded but as it was the boat was nowhere near full. Most of the deck passengers had found themselves canvas deck-loungers and looked far more comfortable than we were, but we had not known the system (very few of the seats in our pullman lounge had been booked). From our deck table we saw a magnificent sunset, and as the water was very calm we watched the headland near to Ancona for a long time as it retreated. It really was a lovely evening.

I think our big mistake on boarding the boat was not to take our lilos and sleeping bags from our bikes; the aircraft-type seats on *The Kydon* were far less comfortable than those of the Bretagne and once again it was necessary to sleep on the floor. We really should have had more foresight, there were not even blankets provided this time, so we had absolutely nothing to pad the hard floor. It was a very bone-stiffening as well as bone-shaking business trying to get a night's sleep (this ferry also transmitted the vibrations far more noticeably). Peter found a set of seats upturned on the lounge floor which he occupied for a while but the gaps in them made for uncomfortable attempts at sleep. However, the following morning, not one but two bodies crawled out from the tiny cramped space which these seats afforded. During the night a German couple had spotted the empty make-shift bunk and moved in, it cannot have been comfortable. Again I had slept on the floor, but this time between two rows of seats to avoid being trodden on.

The adventure was not over yet; we still had another country to see although there was maybe just a little sadness that we would not be cycling it. One thing that had surprised us about our night on the boat was how cold I became during the night, I had to go searching for some of Peter's spare clothes to put on. How we ached in the morning! Thankfully the bar started serving cups of tea good and early, as that was what we wanted more than anything else in the world when we awoke, and for the first time we were not able to light our gas. By the time we went on deck, we must have been in mid-Adriatic, as there was nothing to see on either site of the ferry. We had most of the day to spend on board, we were just so unused to being so idle. We hoped we might pass close to the 'heel' of Italy so we could have one last glimpse but we must have seen the last of the country the previous night. Our next landfall was the coast of Albania just before lunch, soon followed by our first sighting of Corfu.

We found it very interesting steaming down the channel between Corfu and the mainland of Greece as we had been to Corfu two years previously and had taken a boat trip to Albania. We recognised Saranda, the town in Albania which we had visited and Kassioppi, the village in north-eastern Corfu where we had stayed. We also picked out Mount Pantekrator, Corfu's highest mountain, which we had climbed to see the monastery on the summit.

Entering the harbour at lgoumenitsa, we were surprised at what a small town it was, though obviously an important ferry port. Several large ferries were using the harbour, both leaving and entering as well as a couple tied up as we arrived at about 4pm As we wheeled our bikes off the boat into yet another country, we were looking out for signs of or to a campsite but could see none. Peter had the brilliant idea of asking someone at the harbour, to be told it was only one hundred metres up the road, hidden behind a taverna (where better?).

How conveniently everything had fitted into place over the last thirty-six hours. First the ease of getting to Ancona and finding the port, then the incredible way in which we found ourselves boarding the ferry, the relaxation of the ferry crossing and to cap it all a campsite so near the harbour. We could even see the ferries tied up by the quay from the site! It seemed that when the going had been hard, it was all worthwhile and now that we had reached Greece we were going to relax bit and perhaps have a holiday for a couple of weeks, before working out how to get home.

Our many nights of camping wild had paid dividends. We had enough money left over to spend a bit on hiring a car which we knew would be expensive; however, we felt we had earned it. The harbourside at Igoumnenitsa was lined with ferry offices and some of these offered car hire so it did not take long to get ourselves fixed up with a smart little black Séat hatchback, which would enable us to dismantle the bikes and carry them with us. The hire operator offered to store them but we were reluctant to let them out of our sight after such faithful service.

The campsite made up for in convenience what it lacked in comfort and space. We were lucky enough to be able to pick a spot under the trees, the ground was hard and the space minimal (especially after a German guitarist came and pitched very close to our tent, but thankfully he did not stay up playing too late). The facilities were a bit basic but we had not expected luxury, Greek campsites were a completely unknown quantity to us. We found good showers even if the doors did not close properly and one had to hang onto the catch to avoid company! It was certainly a great deal better than many of the sites we had visited, I suppose by this time we felt we were connoisseurs.

It was very pleasant to find familiar items in the shops, for instance the 1.5 litre bottles of Tsantali wine we had enjoyed on previous visits to Greece. We replaced Peter's sandals which I had left behind in Assisi, but unfortunately the *weetabix* we tried to buy was out of date and the shopkeeper had no more.

The camp filled up during the evening as more ferries came in, we could see and hear the boats arriving from our tent. We later learned that this is one of the main entry points for travellers from Europe; even though it is such a small town some quite large transports pass through. We watched another colourful sunset over the harbour and the hills of Corfu. Although the campsite was ruled by a fierce little old woman who had difficulty in walking and frightened off those she did not want by threatening them with exorbitant fees, the town had a very friendly atmosphere due to its small size.

Flash, rumble, rumble, patter went the announcement of our "Welcome to Greece" on Wednesday morning as we looked out of the tent to see a continuous and still growing puddle between us and the washhouse. We remembered that the west coast of Greece is much greener than the rest of the country, we also recalled the spectacular lightning storms we had seen over the area on our holiday in Corfu. They were obviously not restricted to autumn; it was a lovely June morning and we were awash. It did not take very long to strike camp, what a contrast it was to hurl everything into a capacious car rather than easing things into soggy panniers, what luxury. After a stop in the town to cash some money in the bank, which was ankle-deep in rainwater, we were off to the hills towards the centre of the country.

Our stay in Greece is far harder to describe than the previous part of the expedition as it then became a question of description from the inside of a motor car rather than the countryside as seen from the saddle. Still we did try to use our cyclist's eye to view the country – especially when considering the terrain.

It was only a matter of a few minutes before we were right out in the country and heading north-east on the excellent E90-92. This was a really green and beautiful country area, very well covered with wild flowers and flowering shrubs. We just had time to appreciate these before we started to climb. The road became a series of hairpin bends up and then down again – we had entered the mountains and were finding it very much easier than our previous encounters with them.

We were out of the rain, into the sunshine and oh so glad that our bikes were travelling behind and not beneath us!

The car owner had provided us with a good road map of Greece and we were able to plan a route to Meteora easily. By lunchtime we had covered eighty-three kilometres (actually only ten more than our record when cycling, but not over this type of terrain) and had crossed the first mountain range. Old habits dying hard, we stopped for lunch in a place by the road and automatically assessed its suitability as a wild campsite. In fact we had seen plenty of lovely places where a tent could have been pitched as long as we could have found the required few square metres of level ground. All around us here were great green grasshoppers and hooded crows, the latter looking like jackdaws in their tropical khaki. There were the occasional villages clinging to the hillsides, but otherwise it was completely deserted, wild and beautiful. The high spot of the afternoon (excusing the pun) was the Ketara Pass at 1690 metres. All the way up we had seen snow warning signs and two signboards stating that the pass was now open. As we neared it, we noticed the snow depth poles and just a few kilometres beyond, a snow clearing station. It seemed a little odd that a summer holiday destination like Greece could require such precautions but this was the greatest altitude we had reached, albeit with mechanical help.

We did see a pair of cyclists that day, beyond the pass, fully loaded as we had been; they did make us feel briefly a little wimpish, but only briefly. They appeared to be strong blond Germans; we too could have done it, but who knows how many days it would have taken us to cover the distance we had made in just a few hours? For their sake we were pleased to note the drinking water taps we saw along the mountain roads.

Meteora, what a magical-looking place! We had been told of this fascinating place in northern Greece by a friend before setting out. She had described the monastery-crowned hills rising like pinnacles out of the country and had recommended we visit it if at all possible. Still, we were not prepared for how magnificent these pinnacles would be, seen from a distance sticking up like rocky fingers from the plain, each one surmounted by a monastery which appeared to be growing out of it like a fingernail. The town Kastraki which had grown up around them was a resort but not overly so; it offered a choice of campsites and the one we chose was almost beneath one of the largest monasteries. What a contrast to the previous night's site; this one was highly organised, a table and chairs were available, the showers were luxurious and there was even hot water for the washing up!

Such creatures of habit were we, that as soon as the tent was pitched we had the kettle on and were sitting down to review the day and plan the next. We agreed the decision to hire the car had been correct. It was not that the time factor was really important but we were now looking forward to seeing Greece and then going home. We had still not definitely decided how we were going to travel home but the idea of going directly from Corfu was appealing. Had we planned to be 'Round the Worlders' this feeling would not have occurred but we did not fancy being 'Back Trackers'. We toasted our friend Mardie with our tea for suggesting Meteora as a destination. Had we not come here we would not have seen such magnificent countryside – we had not realised before that Greece had these gems. Had we decided to cycle up to Meteora it would have taken several days; we would have had to camp wild and provision accordingly. We had passed very little in the way of civilisation en route. However, one must not forget that officially camping wild is illegal in Greece – it could have been very awkward, though we might have found a few hostels.

Feeling in need of some exercise, we set off to explore the village on foot, to find there was only one bakery nearby and this late in the day it had run out of bread. We were not short of food, but some fresh bread and milk would have been very welcome. So we would just have to decide to eat in the camp restaurant for our evening meal. I was looking forward to my first moussaka for some years and it turned out to be a wise choice, as it arrived soon after we had placed the order. Not so Peter's chicken and chips; the chips were brought but after nearly a quarter of an hour of waiting for the chicken we managed to attract the waiter's attention to ask for the latter. "No chicken", said the waiter though he had accepted the order. We tried again but with no joy so called the manager over. He managed to explain that only the items on the menu with inked in prices were available; the question as to why the waiter had accepted the order was not resolved. We had to wait for a pork chop to be cooked which did not arrive until long after I had finished my moussaka and it quite spoilt our cosy little restaurant dinner. Never mind, we had our own bottle of wine, some fruit and crisps back in the tent where we could sit and watch camp life in comfort.

The first half of the following morning was spent in visiting the largest monastery, the Great Meteoron, just over five minutes drive from the site. Arriving just before it was due to open, we thankfully watched a coachload of Americans depart as they had been to view this one from the outside before going on to see inside another. As we waited for opening time we watched the cable truck being hauled over the abyss. Bags of cement were loaded into a large wooden box and hauled across, we wondered whether the builders themselves used this route or climbed the 154 steps. Our information leaflet said there were 115 uneven steps up to the door of Great Meteoron but we counted 154! From the entrance we could see the windlass point; when the monasteries were built and for centuries after, access was by windlass and bucket only.

The following is a précis of the information sheet we received at the campsite, I include it for general interest:

"The Meteora monasteries rise out of the Thessalian plain in the centre of Greece. Etched by time they appear as nature's gift to the pious, who, driven by faith, have opted for a life of solitude and worship. They have corniced rooftops, wooden galleries and hang precariously over the sinister abysses seeming to grow out of their rocky pinnacles.

During the ninth century, hermits settled in the caves; by the eleventh their numbers had grown and they became communities and during the fourteenth – the first monasteries were established. Douploni and Stagi were the first and in the middle of the century the Great Meteoron was founded by John Uresis, grandson of a prince of Serbia who became the monk Joseph and endowed it richly. During the next two hundred years, the number of monasteries increased to twenty-four, each atop its own little pinnacle. Though many are now in ruins or deserted, they are an amazing sight arising from the plain as one approaches the area. Only five are now inhabited, three by monks and two by nuns. They can all be visited at various times".

I found the inside of the Great Meteoron rather gloomy and forbidding though we could only see a part of it. The magnificent church was at its centre, it was full of gilded lamps and painted icons and staffed by the oldest monk I have ever seen. The outer part of the church was an illustrated story of persecution, the walls covered with the most horrific frescoes depicting tortures and sacrifice and liberally highlighted with red paint. There was an interesting museum containing vestments and bibles of ancient parchment and another containing agricultural implements (though there was no explanation as to how these were used on bare rock) and also a stuffed wolf. Most gruesome was the little 'cemetery room', where the charred bones of the monks were kept; as it is impossible to bury the deceased, they are stored (after semi-cremation) in boxes with the skulls lined up on shelves. The part I liked the most was a peaceful, sunlit courtyard planted with potted geraniums and herbs.

Before leaving we saw the windlass and bucket previously used to keep the monastery supplied. It was quite awe-inspiring to think that all the materials used to build it had been brought up in this manner, after the first monks had presumably scaled the heights and secured rope ladders!

As we left to drive back down to Kastrakis we kept stopping to look at the other monasteries perched on their rocky turrets and marvel at the faith that had driven the monks to build and live in such surroundings. Back on the pilgrimage trail, we set off to search for Philippi. A map in a borrowed Bible Atlas at home showed that we should find it just north of Kavala, so we would follow signs for that town when we found them. As we crossed the plain of Thessalia to Thessaloniki we were once more in the footsteps of St Paul; we had missed out Rome but hoped, after Philippi to travel via Corinth. Alas Ephesus was out for this expedition. (I think the Epistle to the Ephesians is my favourite, but this will have to be the subject of a future journey).

The plain of Thessalia appeared to be a mainly agricultural area, vast acres of grain and fields of beans all being irrigated as we passed. We felt this stretch of the road would be quite easily cyclable, whereas the previous day's would have been a different matter. We were following a continuation of the E92 we had taken out of Igoumenitsa, which had we wanted to, would have taken us all the way down to the Volos Peninsula on the eastern coast. However we left it at Larissa and joined the E75, a toll road which seemed to be the motorway equivalent, joining Athens with Thessaloniki. Just before leaving Larissa we saw a stork's nest perched on top of a church tower, with four young clearly visible from the road.

After a short distance the E75 entered the gorge of the Piniois river which rises near to Meteora and flows into the sea near the site of the ancient town of Tembi. The gorge was very picturesque, wooded and cool. After fifteen kilometres the vegetation thinned out and more rocky outcrops appeared as it neared the sea. We did not see Tembi but we did start to see signs for campsites which pleased us as it proved the accuracy of our map. We chose to stay at Methoni, halfway between Katerini and Thessaloniki, which would give us a good chance of reaching Philippi in the early afternoon of the next day. We had driven over two hundred kilometres in one day, mostly on very good roads, our first real experience of Greek roads, and we were favourably impressed.

This campsite was the first of several we were to stay on at the edge of the main railway line to Athens which has a frequent and noisy service. Several of the sites are really close to the line, on one it passes between the gate and the camping area. Greek trains always seemed to use their hooters as warning of approach to level crossings (of which there are many and they are close together), so we always knew right round the clock when there was a train coming. It was not a very restful night and we were on the road early. The first amusing sight we passed was a restaurant with an aeroplane on its roof, we could think of no explanation other than it was an unusual signboard but it made something worth looking at. Thessaloniki is the largest town in the north of Greece, a large port and commercial town – it appeared to us a rather ugly urban sprawl. It was here we turned again onto the E90, where we saw the first signs for Kavala, that meant a bit more excitement as we knew we were nearing our furthest point.

Once on the E90, we were quickly out into the countryside. The road took us alongside the two lakes which divide the peninsula holding the three fingers of Halkidiki onto the rest of Greece. Kavala was another port, albeit a smaller one, but it proved a busy and confusing town to try to navigate through. We were a bit upset that we could not find any signs to Philippi, but by a bit of deft map-reading and some good fortune, found and followed the sign to Drama, which appeared to be in the right direction. On the outskirts of Kavala, this was confirmed by a sign that told us we were only ten kilometres from our goal.

Arriving at Philippi we now felt very excited; we had reached the furthest point of the expedition. Philippi is a ruined town with no present-day building other than a restaurant which was not open. We came across the town quite suddenly, and typically for us, it was just as it started to rain. We English, we cannot go anywhere without our own private rain-showers; we had even visited the Acropolis in Athens some years before in a thunderstorm.

Quite an extensive Roman site, Philippi stretches both sides of the modern road and we could enter from either side. The thing that was missing was a guide book, so we had to content ourselves with buying the five available postcards and hunting out the sights from these. Our new organist back at home had told us about St Paul's cell and one of the cards was of this, so we were able to find it; a cramped 'room' where St Paul is reputed to have been kept prisoner for some years, with barely enough room to lie down. We also picked our way over the ruins of the early Christian church, several columns of which are still standing, along with parts of the walls. We walked amongst what must have been the streets and houses of the first century town, it was with awe and appreciation of the stillness and isolation that we made that visit; such a contrast from the bustle and noise when we visited Jerusalem, where one cannot tread quite the same ground that Christ trod because of the change in earth levels[3]. There was a great sense of achievement on reaching the town where St Paul spent so much time, even if it was not a happy time. This was a place like no other where I felt one could come close to the roots of Christianity; it was also remarkable that it was all so accessible. Coming from a country where everything at interesting archaeological sites is so often fenced off, I found it amazing that we could just wander all over the site. The only part we could not see was a great mosaic floor which was fenced and locked.

---

[3] Due to the earthquakes and subsequent rebuilding, the present day streets of Jerusalem are several metres higher than they were two thousand years ago; only at Bethlehem, in the crypt of the Church of the Nativity, were we at the original level of the stable.

Chapter 14   After Philippi

Our feelings as we left Philippi were hard to describe, we felt tremendously fulfilled as we had reached our goal but that is an understatement. Perhaps we were a little disappointed that we arrived in a car but the important thing was - we had made it! Although the town itself was not quite as impressive as we had hoped it would be, it represented a milestone in our lives; it was the furthest point in our journey and after this journey we would neither of us be the same people as before. It also represented something rather special in our Christian faith which I do not have the words to describe.

After Philippi, we travelled another eighty-eight kilometres that day, retracing the road past the lakes. At Asprovita we found the campsite Europa, a large and sophisticated site where the pitches were marked off by individual hedges and the whole site like a great garden with even our own flock of ladybirds. That night I wrote in my travel diary - "We are somewhat confused, having passed the furthest point, we are looking forward to going home, but though a part of each of us is feeling homesick, another part is so used to travelling that there is a wish to go on. We expect to feel severe withdrawal symptoms when we finally reach home and the expedition is all over. It is probably best to go home while we still have a strong desire to see more of the world; we have both been thoroughly bitten by the travelling bug, but we realise that such an opportunity is unlikely to come our way again. It is surely best that this remains a unique experience".

On our fourth day of driving, we visited the most easterly of the 'three fingers' of Halkidiki. We had been fascinated by the indication on the map that this little peninsula seemed to be covered with monasteries so we thought it would be an interesting place to visit. The road only went as far as Ouranopoli and the drive to it was incredibly beautiful. Green wooded hillsides to feed the charcoal industry, the evidence of which was all around us (especially in the nostrils) and included the man by the road trying to sell us little black bundles. The fairly gentle hills would have made really pleasant cycling and we were very impressed with the spectacular views which greeted us as we swept around corners and looked over lovely bays. At the end of the road was a tourist town with buses disgorging day-trippers and a car ferry crossing the Kolpos from the second finger, but no sign of any monasteries. Not that we intended to make any more visits to them, we were just intrigued by the vast number shown on the map and had expected to see so many but they must have been well hidden away in the trees. It had been a very worthwhile drive to see such a picturesque, unspoilt part of Greece.

We spent the remainder of the day returning via Thessaloniki to the section of the coast where there were numerous campsites on our way to the Corinth canal. The site we chose turned out to be one of the most expensive. In the town of Platamos, it was just below a castle which, by the time we had climbed the hill to see it, was closed for the night. However there were excellent views over the Thermaikos Kolpos as the castle must have been built to guard Thessaloniki. This was the first site where we had found a beach which provided lovely clear water for an evening swim, very refreshing after a hot day behind the wheel. We had covered 318 kilometres and it had been impossible to find shade beside the road for a lunch stop. Instead we had to drive a short distance off the road and park on the edge of a cliff, where we could watch the sea, the birds and the insects. The other direction looked over towards Mount Olympus. It seemed that once on the motorway, the requirement is to keep going and the few pull-ins were not for stopping for more than a few minutes as shady trees were in very short supply. At this stage we were trying to cover as much distance as possible and were so glad we had hired the car. Our ambitions would have been seriously curtailed had we tried to see Greece by bike, we just could not have seen such widely spread sights.

Sunday morning saw us gazing over the Corinth canal from the road bridge. Though I had seen it some years before, I was still amazed by its depth and sheer sides. We stayed to watch a cruise ship passing below us; it was being towed by a minute tug which was having a difficult job to keep its burden from bumping into the sides of the canal as there was very little room to manoeuvre. We found it, quite alarming standing on the bridge as every time a lorry went over the whole structure shook considerably. Either side of the bridge were car parks for the sight-seers, plentifully stocked with souvenir shops but we gave those a miss.

After Corinth came our 'two day wild goose chase'. We had intended to drive along the southern shore of the Gulf of Corinth, take the ferry at the western end and continue up the west coast of Greece to Levkas. Having spent a peaceful Sunday night away from the trains and beside a pretty part of the coast, we arrived at the ferry port to find everything at a standstill. We could see all the ferries tied up along the quayside and a collection of cars and drivers waiting but no-one seemed to know what was going on. We attempted to consult the port police but it was from an English hitchhiker that we discovered there was a ferry strike and nothing was going to move that day. No, he did not know whether the next port along, Egio, about twenty-five kilometres back, was operating, but there was nothing for it but to go and find out. Well, of course, no ferries were operating from there either but we did understand from the strikers that the strike was for forty-eight hours and there would be no movement for two days.

It was a long and hot drive back around the Gulf of Corinth and it took us over twenty-four hours to reach the point where the ferry should have arrived after a fifteen minute crossing! Such is life; we could not afford to wait the forty-eight hours as we had less than a week left before we had to return the car and there were other places we wanted to see on the Ionian coast. The drive around the north coast of the Gulf of Corinth was very interesting as the roads after Livadia became less well used and navigation a bit more challenging. For the most part, the signs were in Greek only and our map was all in English. Some of the letters in the Greek alphabet look similar to ours but do not always equate so I had to give myself a quick crash course in learning the Greek alphabet, taught only by the signposts, which made knowing where we were going a great adventure. In this area of more minor roads which were not numbered, we did not even have that to help us. We were also confused by the road markings, where we found them; what appeared to be the main road was often not that at all. The scenery was ever changing, steep sharp turns in the road giving us new and increasingly lovely panoramas. Near to Itea, the rock and earth turned a rust red and it looked as if there had been mining. This was reinforced by seeing the number of ships in the gulf of Itea, although most of them looked unemployed. There was even one in the shallows which appeared to be leaning up against the deserted harbour wall.

One more day of driving and we reached Levkas; almost an island, it is joined to the mainland by a causeway guarded by castles. It is fairly hilly and wonderfully green as we had discovered much of the west of Greece to be. We inspected three sites before settling on one about halfway between Lefkada and Nidri (the capital and one of the holiday centres). Although the site was a bit basic, it was certainly adequate for a two night stay. We had lunch under the shade of some olive trees watching large brown butterflies which, when settled, looked just like dead leaves but in flight showed patterns of cream-speckled brown. It was so peaceful here, we pitched the tent under some lemon trees with a donkey by the fence to give us our morning call.

Later that afternoon we reassembled the bikes and rode to Nidri to see what the town had to offer. It seemed strange to be in the saddle again after a week, but it felt very good, especially as we were minus panniers. Nidri was a real tourist trap – expensive looking boats moored up in the harbour and ships taking day-trippers. Everywhere there were restaurants trying to entice us in and souvenir shops plentifully sprinkled all around. We saw a couple of supermarkets, but decided to give them a miss in favour of the ones nearer our campsite which we felt might not have such a high tourist mark-up. It was a very pleasant afternoon ride, the scenery was really worth coming to see and we had a late-afternoon breeze for welcoming coolness. We thought we would treat ourselves to a meal out the following evening, either at Nidri or Lefkada, the town we would be surveying the next morning. We made a stop at Nikiana (just over one kilometre from the site) for some milk and really cold beer, then we had to race 'home' before it warmed up.

Supper included another of our culinary experiments – fresh green beans which had been quite easy to carry in the car. After that we set out to walk off our meal and to discover the nearby beach. It was small and deserted, but for a lone fisherman searching, we thought, for octopus. We are not lovers of sandy beaches and this was a good one, all pebbles which gave us a chance to indulge in our favourite beach occupation, sorting through a handful of pebbles examining the colours and veining. The following day we returned there for a gentle swim, lazily floating in the water and watching the boats cruising up and down the sound. If I am trying to make this island sound idyllic, I must be forgiven – it was. Apart from Nidri it was very peaceful, the views were good and the water ideal.

In the morning we were greeted by a triple alarm call. At approximately 7 am, three donkeys from three different directions started to greet each other and the world at the top of their voices – I am sure God created donkeys without volume controls. Otherwise the site was very quiet, only one other family of campers in a caravan and a couple of 'dummy' tents. We decided to spend the morning visiting Lefkada, the island's main town, as we hoped to find a bank. Lefkada appeared to be a mixture of commerce and tourism, the harbour accommodated both fishing boats and pleasure yachts, the shops likewise were both souvenir and grocery shops. The whole town had a pleasant atmosphere, several of the streets had fruit and vegetable stalls and these were very busy as I went on my by now daily search for peaches and apricots.

After our pre-lunch swim and a light cheese and fruit lunch, we decided to conserve our energy under the lemon trees for an hour or so – we were having no difficulty relaxing in Greece. In the early evening we rode again to Nidri to have a tourist-style supper in one of the waterfront restaurants. The owners were all touting for custom as we walked up and down trying to compare almost identical menus. Eventually we settled on the one where the Michael Jackson look-alike owner promised us a free bottle of local wine with our meal. It was most relaxing to sit sipping our beer and watching the boats going to and fro. One was a very unusual looking day cruise boat, built to resemble an ancient galley with very high bow and stern and painted a garish blue. There were several expensive looking yachts tied up near us; Peter recognised one as being of the type he used to build some years ago. As we ate our garlic mushrooms, moussaka and steak, we were entertained by a family of maidens having their showers on deck from a black 'hot water-bottle-tank' tied to the mast. We had seen several of these on campsites, a large black rubber bag tied to a tree, gathering the solar warmth to give the camper a warm shower at the end of the day. I just wished we had had such luxuries when I used to sail, in those days all we had was a flannel and cold water.

It was obvious why Levkas is such a popular holiday venue. The view across the channel to Skorpios and Kalamos is spectacular and in June everything is still so very green. Friday, 25th June was our final day of driving, when we left Levkas to return to Igoumenitsa. We noted the castles guarding the causeway to the mainland and commented on the lack of ruins and antiquities in this part of the country considering the length of its history. We could only imagine that with wars and the probable need for building materials, most of the stone has been moved or used subsequently. We caught the ferry to Preveza with no delay and drove past the airport that brings the holidaymakers to the area. Obviously a very small airport, nothing like its big sister at Corfu, and we saw only a couple of aircraft.

We felt a special need to revisit Parga, a pretty harbour town halfway between Preveza and Igoumenitsa. We first came to it on our very first holiday in Greece, the year we spent a week on Paxos, the Ionian island after which we named our house. Parga is a particularly beautiful natural harbour surmounted by a castle above crystal clear water. The hills drop majestically into the sea and there are three tiny islets which help to provide shelter from the westerly winds. The harbour area, although looking a little cleaner, was unchanged, and we quickly wound our way through the streets to walk up to the castle to see the views. Again the castle grounds were full of brown butterflies enjoying the sun, and the smell of warm herbs was just as we remembered. We had the castle almost to ourselves, only a few others were enjoying the sights with us so we felt very relaxed. It was quite surprising to see that some repairs were in progress, as there was no entrance fee charged. There must have been concerts in the evenings, as there were stacks of chairs on the terrace, part of the ramparts forms a natural stage. I imagine the atmosphere would be perfect for Peer Gynt or Wagner. Back down at the town level we bought a few postcards before returning to the car to chase away the children who were running their toy cars over the bonnet.

Another forty kilometres or so over the steep hilly roads, and we were back at Igoumenitsa for lunch. The drive that morning had been one of the most impressive of all. Most of the time we had been on the E55, one of the main roads of western Greece, so the surface had been good but the road had been very steep and in places it was very twisty. The car had carried us just over 2,500 kilometres through the mainland and a great variety of countryside. It had really been worth hiring the car, as we realised we would have covered only a very small fraction of the country on our bicycles, but at least they had travelled with us. It had certainly been the comfortable way of seeing the country and we felt we deserved it. Fortunately we had been fairly frugal and of course we were reducing our time away, so we felt the additional cost justifiable.

The final weekend of our expedition was spent mainly at the campsite at Igoumenitsa, a conveniently situated if not luxurious base. It was convenient for the ferry to Corfu, it was convenient for the town's shops and as for entertainment there was always the harbour as well as the coming and goings of the site. On our first evening we met an Australian couple who only stayed a short while. We do not know whether Madame disliked Australians or just this couple, but she quoted him the exorbitant fee of 5,500 drachmas for the night whereupon they made a cup of tea and had a think, a few quick calculations and conversions into their own currency and then drove off. Later on we saw them parked near the harbour, cooking their steaks for supper, so we stopped for a chat. They told us what had happened and how they would stay there for the night as long as they were not moved on and leave early in the morning. At least with a motor caravan they could be completely self-contained and stay in a car park if necessary. This couple had been all over the Middle and Near East; Syria, Turkey and Jordan to name a few and were making their way back to London to sell their van before flying back to Australia.

It was just getting dark so we hung on to watch the ferries light up and leave, four went out in procession sailing into a most colourful sunset. As the sun sank below the hills of Corfu, the sky turned all imaginable shades of pink, purple and gold. The evening's entertainment was provided by the Paxos ferry. We soon realised there must have been some roadbuilding work in progress as we watched a road-roller, a small JCB and a large caterpillar vehicle on a low-loader line up beside the little blue ferry boat. As we arrived and took our ringside seat on a bollard the roller moved aboard followed by the JCB. There were then about twenty-five crew and hangers-on shouting instructions and generally offering verbal help. The low-loader advanced up the gangway but proved too tall to fit through the deck doorway so had to back down. After a bit of head-scratching the captain ordered it to be turned round and try to reverse in, but this time the cab scraped the top and left behind some yellow paint before being halted by the doorway. Next a couple of lorries were taken off but even that did not help. We noticed that as the lorries were unloaded the boat rose a little making the angle less steep and providing more headroom. Peter went over and suggested to the 'boss' that they unload all the lorries and try again but as it was getting late he did not want to do this. So they next unloaded the 'cat' from the low loader, and with a great deal of scraping and noise drove the latter aboard. It was a perfect fit, all they had to do was drive the cat back into position and sail off. Alas, it could only get part way onto the loader, as once again the roof of the cab fouled the deck doorway. By now the crowd of spectators had increased several fold as had the shouting and the poor driver must have been tearing out his hair as he was told to unload the whole caboodle onto the quayside. The two lorries were then replaced and the ferry sailed off into the night leaving the 'cat', loader and the disconsolate driver who disappeared, probably into the nearest bar. We felt very sorry for him, he seemed to know it was not going to fit and he was being so terribly embarrassed by all the well-intentioned and voluble advisers. The following day we saw, parked on the quay, the loader with cat, which had had its cab removed and placed in the front of the loader – how simple!

On Saturday we caught the mid-morning ferry over to Corfu. We were very excited as we were going to find a travel agent who would arrange to get us home. We were still not sure by what mode of transport we would make the journey but we were quite open-minded, the only conclusion we had come to was that we would not be cycling (at least not very much). Would it be a cross-European coach, a flight to Bristol, a tramp-steamer or cargo ship? We were at the stage of being prepared for anything as long as we could take the bikes. We pedalled into the centre of Corfu until we came to the 'Street of Many Travel Agents'. There were so many to choose from but we settled on one that had English posters in the window. After a quick explanation to the manager, he phoned one of his airline brokers. "Bristol? No chance, but you can go to Glasgow, Manchester or Stansted, but I'd advise you to sell your bikes here." We explained that the deal was to get us and the bikes back to the UK and with either of those airports we would still have several days travelling ahead of us, so we needed our transport. He agreed, and half an hour later we came out with a piece of paper confirming a flight on Tuesday morning (well, the middle of Monday night) and several traveller's cheques lighter. A mile across town to collect our tickets from the broker and we were all set; well almost, we still had to find some cardboard to wrap our 'luggage', to protect against any possible damage to our precious bicycles.

We were so pleased it had all been accomplished so easily, we now had single tickets to Stansted, at a very good price and booked so quickly. We still had to find out exactly where Stansted was in relation to home but we knew it was in Essex, so must be in the right half of England. We also realised that London stood between the airport and home but that was three days away. Now we just had two days to kill fairly gently, before the long journey home. The ferry journey from Corfu to the mainland takes just under two hours so we were back well before tea time. We were in very high spirits, as although we had just completed the most amazing experience of our lives, we were now eager to be on our way home. Over the last twenty-four hours we had spent far more money than on the whole of the rest of the trip, by paying for the car hire and the airline tickets. We were so glad we had saved the traveller's cheques and had used our Visa cards and 'holes-in-the-walls' for our living expenses.

Sunday being our last full day, we decided to spend it exploring the locality of Igoumenitsa, so we pedalled off to the western end of the bay where we found another and more expensive looking campsite beside a tourist beach. Barely eight kilometres from the harbour and town, the beach was equipped with pedalos and surf-skis and was obviously a playground for the locals. We sat under the trees and ate ice creams before a lazy ride back. I suppose we were now getting used to the heat; though we had done so little cycling recently, as long as we kept the distances down we experienced no problems. We also found it blissful without our heavy loads, so we made the most of our last day of riding without them.

The problem now was to find some cardboard boxes to make up bike packaging. All the shops were closed when we went looking in the afternoon but as we crossed one street I happened to see a piece of cardboard on top of a skip. Close investigation revealed a quantity of clean, flattened, large cardboard boxes which when cut and taped would provide all we would need. Were we being looked after? We spent an hour on site measuring, cutting and marking and the next day bought some heavy quality parcel tape. These pieces, neatly rolled on the backs of our panniers accompanied us to the airport on Monday afternoon.

On Sunday evening we met an English couple on the site who showed us their Road Atlas of Britain and helped us plan a route from Stansted to Devon. We could expect three or four days of cycling back across England. It always seemed to amaze me that so many of the English people we met came from places we know. Frances, co-owner of the atlas, came from Honiton, through which we would pass in a few days' time. Also on our final night in Igoumenitsa, we met an Italian cycling couple just off the ferry who were resting for the night before setting off to ride to Meteora. Their spirit of adventure made us feel a little wimpish, so before watching them set out we showed them on their map the locations of the water taps we had noted on our way there. We commented on the fact they were several years our junior and of course we had ridden right through Europe to get here, which made us feel a bit better as we waved them good-bye. They made a colourful picture as they cycled away on pink and purple bikes with clothing and panniers to match.

So we came to our last day in Greece. By this time we were so excited by the prospect of flying home that we hardly had time to feel any sadness that our nomadic lifestyle was about to undergo a complete change, and the withdrawal symptoms we were to feel were still several days away. We spent the morning shopping for food to last us until the flight, a lunch to be cooked at the campsite and a picnic supper to eat in the park in Corfu town, thus reversing the pattern of eating we had stuck to so rigidly for the past three months. We also had to pack things a little differently so that we could use the paired front panniers as cabin baggage and dispose of any excess before striking camp. Although the flight was not due to take off until the early hours of the following morning, we had to travel over and make for the airport before dark. So eager were we to be on the move that after an early cooked lunch we set off to catch the 2.30pm ferry arriving in Corfu at teatime, but alas we could no longer make tea. As one cannot carry gas cylinders on the plane, we had used up our remaining gas at lunch time and had to content ourselves with water and the last of the wine for tea and supper. Buying an English newspaper to while away the hours in the park, we set about a relaxing few hours doing our homework, trying to catch up with some at the political goings on that had happened whilst we had been away. We saw several backpackers sitting in the park, presumably awaiting their turn to go to the airport, just like us. We were actually only a short distance from the airport as we discovered when, as the light began to fade, we set off in the direction indicated by the excellent sign-posting. As we turned our backs on the harbour we did feel some regret, I think it was then we realised that we were actually leaving Greece, which we had always found so welcoming. We love the warmth, the scenery, the sunsets and relaxation of this country.

We cycled into Corfu airport at 8pm feeling very alien to all the other travellers arriving in cars, taxis and coaches. We must have looked quite amusing with our rolls of cardboard tied on top of our panniers and our almost empty bag of food and bottle of wine dangling from the sides. Our check-in time was not until 1 am, but we wanted to be through the streets before dark so we had to settle down to quite a long wait. Corfu airport is not the most comfortable for several hours of sitting around, but it was far less crowded than Paphos, in Cyprus, which had been our most recent experience. At least there was plenty going on for us to watch. By midnight we had finished the wine and crisps and thought lovingly of our lilos and tent; normally we would have been tucked up and asleep for a couple of hours by then.

Suddenly it was time to dress up the bikes in their cardboard overalls and this actually took longer than we had anticipated. The only dismantling we did was to reverse the pedals and turn the handlebars through ninety degrees. Although we had heard conflicting advice about deflating tyres to avoid bursting, the latest advice was only to deflate a little, so this we did. While Peter finished wrapping tape around our strange looking packages, I found the Unijet representative who had been warned about us. She escorted us to the check-in desk and watched with us as the bicycles were wheeled away towards the aircraft loading point. Our large panniers pretended to be suitcases and our small ones we zipped together as hand baggage. The transition was so easily accomplished, we were even shepherded to the head of the check-in queue, so we feel that travelling with wheels has a definite advantage – the novelty value to the staff must have been paramount. From the departure lounge we could see the two baggage trolleys each surmounted by a bicycle being towed out to the aircraft. It caused some comments from other passengers; one young man next to me told his friend, "Look, there's a bike on that trolley", the other was disbelieving until I told them it was a bike and it was mine. I suppose some years ago, until I looked into the idea, I would not have believed in flying bikes either. As we walked out to the aircraft, they were being loaded as the last items; it appeared great care was being taken of them.

Just before 3.30am Corfu-time, we were airborne. We could now settle down to a few hours of relaxation and meditation before the shock to our systems of being let loose in England again. We hoped we would be able to catnap a little as we were just not used to going without our much-valued sleep, and we knew we had a long ride ahead of us. We had ridden 5416 kilometres since we left home on 24th March, almost fourteen weeks ago, and we felt justly proud of ourselves.

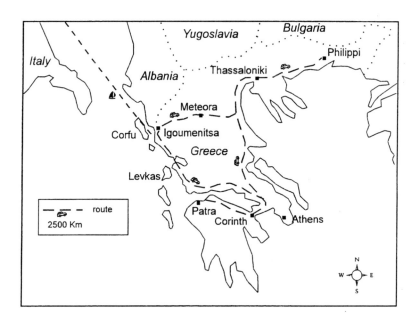

Chapter 15 Homeward

The airline breakfast was served to us at 3 am. (I think it was English time), and just two hours later, wheels touched tarmac at Stansted. It had been a smooth, uneventful flight and here we were at five o'clock in the morning at a hitherto unknown airport (to us). Stansted is very modern and very easy to get through. We had no sooner arrived at the terminal than our 'luggage' was on its way too. Our two bicycles were again carefully wheeled through the doors for us and our panniers came sailing up the carousel. Our cardboard made quite a pile as we extracted our vehicles and prepared them for the onward journey. A kind official said they would remove the cardboard and before we were ready to leave, it had disappeared. One gets strange looks wheeling a fully laden bicycle out of the arrivals' terminal even at that early hour of the morning, but there we were on the road at six o'clock with a newly-purchased map of southern England, trying to find our way towards Devon. We had to remember to ride on the left hand side of the road; lots of cars with English number plates passed us before we realised where we were.

It was so very early and a comparatively cool, slightly misty morning so we started off in track suits. In order to avoid London, we had to aim for Hertford keeping the M25 to the south of us. Neither of us knew this part of England at all, though once we reached Hertfordshire I would know a little better where we were as I had lived there for some years. We had slight hopes of reaching our brother-in-law's house near Basingstoke by the end of the day, though it seemed an awfully long way and our progress would depend on the terrain, and that was the unknown factor.

Once on our way we realised that the first priority would be a decent breakfast; airline meals may be sufficient for the motorist but are totally unsuited to the calorie-burning cyclist. The nearby Little Chef, though claiming to open at seven, was still closed by twenty past so we continued until we found the early-morning-cyclist's dream – a transport café on the outskirts of Hertford, which provided us with a real full-belly breakfast including tea in mugs. We had the works; beans, eggs, mushrooms, bacon, sausage and toast. Thus fortified, we set off again at 9.15am to tackle England.

It was a truly delightful English summer day, the sort which one remembers from childhood picnics, and by avoiding the most heavily-trafficked areas we enjoyed it to the full. Bypassing towns, the signs to Hatfield, St Albans and Hemel Hempstead sped by and we moved into Buckinghamshire, the county of my birth. We lunched in a green lane near Mop End, where we lay on the grass and listened to *The Archers* on our radio! We had expected crossing the Chilterns to be a hard and slow series of climbs, but, as had been with the Apennines, there was just one really steep one at High Wycombe (though hardly in the same category as the Italian mountain pass). By mid-afternoon the water bottles were empty, so I had to go and plead with a roadside café to fill them. The young waiter was so impressed that he gave me the last of the ice from his ice-making machine, hoping he would not incur the wrath of his manager.

After the Chilterns, we turned south to cross the Thames near Marlow and taking the road between Reading and Maidenhead, managed once again to avoid heavy traffic. It amazed me that although so near London, we cycled through such lovely rural areas well away from urbanisation. I suppose we were experiencing the same as in southern Spain, where we had imagined it to be all tower blocks yet found such wonderful areas completely empty of people and buildings. Yes, the world is full of surprises, or maybe we just get such fixed ideas and then wonder why the reality does not live up to them.

After skirting Reading we quickly came to Stratfield Saye, the estate of the Duke of Wellington and his descendants, which is adjacent to Heckfield, where Brian, our brother-in-law lives. We had hoped to find a phone box and give him some warning but we did not find one we could use until we were almost there. We had even thought of phoning and asking him to come and fetch us if we had run out of energy but we somehow managed to find enough of that to complete the necessary 143 kilometres, an overall record distance, an impressive 88½ miles!! It was satisfying to be able to cycle up to his door and give him the surprise of his life. To have us appear on the doorstep quite out of the blue would have floored many a relative, but he just exclaimed "You were in Italy and on your way to Greece when I got your card yesterday". Once again we were taken in and offered floor space for the night, (his nephew was staying in the spare bedroom), just as in the Algarve, and similarly the first thing we were glad to be offered was the good old cup of tea.

Brian quickly arranged to take us out to one of his locals for a meal with his nephew Jolyon. He had given us another marvellous welcome and we even had a chance to phone my parents and give them a few days warning. They too thought we were still in Greece and we could imagine how they would get the bush-telegraph working around the village so that the element of surprise would be lost.

Fortunately it was not one of the days when Brian had to be up at the crack of dawn to go to Covent Garden, so we were able to enjoy a relaxed evening and have a sociable breakfast before setting off again. He invited us to spend a few days with him, but we were afraid that if we stopped before reaching home we would find it harder to do the necessary distances. There were still nearly 200 miles to be covered, which we expected to take about three days and we hoped the weather (far less predictable then we were used to) would stay kind.

Now we were five counties away from home and had a couple more nights to spend camping. The last day of our fourteenth week was all spent on the A30, which we joined at Hook and stayed on in preference to the busier A303, that we usually use when visiting Brian. During the early part of the day we passed through some of the prettiest Hampshire villages, red brick and tiles with colourful roses growing up and over the cottages. For a short stretch the A303 runs concurrently but the heavy traffic was off-putting and we were glad when the roads diverged again. According to our map, the A30 looked more direct although we could expect more hills. It was a road unknown to us both, so it was a bit more of an adventure.

Near Salisbury we stopped for lunch under a railway bridge which offered some trees for a shady siesta. We hoped to camp somewhere near Shaftesbury as that would take us one county nearer home, and cycling right through Wiltshire would add to our satisfaction. Our siesta went on rather longer than intended and it was 3.45pm when we awoke and set off again. The terrain that day had been excellent, far better than we expected, though we knew that when we neared Devon we were in for some hills, several of which we already knew to be steep ones. So we were enjoying this less hilly road while we could. At Ludwell, four miles before Shaftesbury, we found a shop to buy provisions and asked about campsites in the town. The shopkeepers said they were sure there was a site but did not know its whereabouts, so we would have to seek it out for ourselves.

As it happened it was quite difficult to find, as the necessary signs were not evident and we rode right into the town centre before finding that we had passed within a few yards of it. This was because it was a part-time site, being on the edge of a football ground. We could pitch at the edge of the football field very cheaply using their facilities (during their very limited opening hours). We were the only campers and we soon discovered that the outside water supply was not turned on, but this was made up for by being able to fill up from the bar and being able to use the referee's shower in comfort and privacy.

The weather had held so far, so we made an early start before eight o'clock and spent the morning dodging in and out of Dorset, as the A30 crossed the corners of the counties. We were optimistic about reaching the Devon border before the end of the day, so there was no stopping off to sightsee although it would have been good to explore Sherborne castle which we saw from the road. We were surprised to reach Yeovil by mid-morning and it was after this that we began to meet the hills which slowed our progress. We felt our real welcome to the West country was the long hill up to East Chinnock which made for a slow walk. At least the lovely warm sun made the transition back to England less of a shock to the system than it might have been.

I do not think I had ever been up the famous Yarcome Hill before, certainly not at a walk, though we had both heard of it many times on traffic reports. It was long and it was steep but the scenery in the sunlight was distracting us from our aching thighs and calves. Certainly the long run down through Monkton, where we joined the A303 again was cooling and comforting as we returned to more familiar territory. Remembering that the Honiton bypass is a fast and furious road, we were anxious to avoid it, so were delighted to see just before it a welcome campsite sign. Most fortuitous, and the site proved to be a very pleasant one just off the road, well spread out and with a railway line behind. It also had comfortable hot showers, of which we were most in need.

Once we had pitched the tent and cleaned ourselves up, we left off the panniers and went into Honiton for what we hoped was to be our final food shopping of the expedition. We were hit by another wave of excitement, by the next evening we should be home and sleeping in our own bed! We celebrated our final night under canvas with a final bottle of wine watching another wonderful sunset, the fiery red ball slipping away behind English hills for a change.

Honiton at 8.15am had the air of a country town just coming to life in an almost old-fashioned way. I feel sure the town has become more pleasant to live and work in since the bypass took the heavy traffic away from its main street. From there it was a fairly flat road to Exeter, but once we reached there, which way should we go? We had a bit of confusion as all roads seemed to lead towards the M5 but finally we found the road going to the 'alternative' Haldon Hill. Haldon Hill is another famous one to West Country drivers and nowadays is a fast, furious and fume-laden hill which is not pleasant for cyclists. We have negotiated it once but this time preferred to search out the much older though steeper 'road round the back'. This was definitely the steepest hill we encountered in England, it seemed to be one of the steepest of the whole expedition, but that was probably because home was so near. We could see a pair of brightly coloured cyclists ahead of us, but try as we did, we could not quite catch up with them. At the top we found they had halted so we could have a chat. A Dutch couple, they had arrived in Exeter the previous day on a specially-fitted biking holiday bus. They said they were hoping to visit Tintagel in Cornwall during the week before the bus would collect them again. I was most amused to see them the following day in South Brent (our home village) through which they had decided to ride after camping at Ashburton. I was then able to give them directions towards north Cornwall.

Just as a final fling, we had two punctures at the top of Haldon, Peter's back tyre was making its presence felt and after the second flat he changed the outer also. By the time we were whizzing down Haldon we realised we could make it home for a belated lunch. With renewed energy we tackled our last hill, Rattery Hill, within a few miles of home, the last one we had to walk up. We were getting quite hot but the thought of a long beer, even if a bit warm, was beckoning us. We could hardly believe we had brought the hot weather back with us, but as we were so acclimatised to it we hardly noticed the heat.

At 1.40pm precisely we rode into the village without any fanfare; however, riding down Church Street we were recognised by our friend, Lindy, who shouted, "They're back", so we knew we must be.

Our first stop was St Petroc's Church, thankfully empty, just for a few moments of quiet to say "Thank you". Fifteen weeks and two days we had been away and had covered 5,832 kilometres, which equalled 3,615 miles.

Having spent approximately 600 hours in the saddle over the past three months we had an enormous amount of time to reflect, to plan and also it enabled our minds to wander. Towards the end of our trip Peter admitted to me that the one thing that had been a daily mind-jerker to him was the carnage suffered by the domestic animals and wildlife across the five countries we had ridden through. If we had seen such slaughter in just 3,500 miles of roads, how much must the world's highways produce? So he had directed some of his thoughts to composing the following:-

The Wheel

It's said to be the greatest aid mankind has ever seen.
Down through the ages and even now its reign has been supreme.
Made of rubber, stone, or wood, polythene and of steel.
Watch its path, see where it's been, it marks an evil trail.
It smashes a track of pain and death, misery and fear.

In three short months we saw that track;
Bird, weasel, goat, rabbit, dog and cat,
Insect, lizard, snake, rat and beautiful swallowtail butterfly.
Smashed, broken, disembowelled, crushed, just sleeping, their bodies lay in crazy pose.

No longer the wheel in our mind's eye will ever hold its head so high,
And we hope the next mode to progress can tread more softly as it moves
And pray be gentle with our little friends.

Peter Finch July 1993

EPILOGUE

Now that we have been home for a few months we have had time to reflect on all that we have done and that has happened to us, I think that neither of us is quite the same person. We have learned much about ourselves and we each learned about the other in a way that would not have been possible under 'normal' circumstances (and we are still together!). We found that we had endurance we did not expect of people in their forties, even though on occasions we had to force it somewhat; we also learned the length of my fuse! We each feel that we have completed the greatest achievement of our lives, nothing either of us had done hitherto even comes close to measuring up to this expedition. I think we can be justly proud of ourselves.

We discovered that our stereotyped visions of the countries we visited were often wildly inaccurate; for example the great area of wilderness we found in southern Spain where we had expected to see ribbons of high-rise development. Travelling by bicycle, we were able to see countryside from the ground up. We chose bicycles mainly from the economic stance but also for their more leisurely pace where we could really appreciate each area and not flash past without time to notice things. Also we chose them because of their quiet and a wish not to add to pollution. An added bonus that had not really occurred to us beforehand was the flexibility of choosing places to camp – there were times when we completely disappeared into the countryside.

However, we did feel disadvantaged by not having basic knowledge of the languages; it would have added to our experiences had we been able to converse and ask questions along the way. As it was we had to rely on our eyes and in a few places, the knowledge of the English campers we met who had made previous visits, such as at Pisa and Lake Trasimeno.

One good lesson we learned was that we could live fairly comfortably for three months with just what we could carry in our panniers. A single gas cooker, a candle, a tiny radio and a few pocket-sized games made up our luxuries. The best purchase we made before leaving was our rainwear (nearly twice the price of our tent, but worth every penny); it proved absolutely vital during our crossings of the Picos and the Sierra de Ronda. The best purchase during the expedition were the replacement airbeds, we had been getting very aching backs when we were let down so often onto the hard ground. It was during that period we adopted the title of Middle-aged Travellers.

With the benefit of hindsight, what would we have done differently? I think not a lot. There were times during the steepest climbs when I thought it would have been nice to have done it all ten years earlier, but of course that would not have been possible; we had not even met and at that time I was hardly in a fit state to walk without a stick let alone contemplate a bicycle. I think we should have bought larger-scale maps earlier on in the trip. It was not until we were given one by the Dutch/Spanish couple in Mojacar that we realised how beneficial they were, well worth the extra weight. The language I have mentioned, having spent so long in Spain it would have helped if at least one of us had been on a course. We should also have taken slide film; after we returned we went to the considerable expense of transferring some sixty prints onto slides so we could share our experiences with the community. We would also NOT have taken white underwear or T-shirts, the 'Tiger' soap was just not up to getting out the grey!

Now for planning the next expedition. Yes, hopefully there will be several more, but probably of shorter duration. With my earnings of subsequent weeks of temping we bought a lightweight trailer to carry the bulk equipment next time, but more importantly as a water bowser. If we can be independent and carry enough food and water for a few days without having to search out shops with their sometimes (for us anyway) inconvenient opening times, we shall be able to get 'further away from it all'. We hope next to visit eastern Spain again as there is much more we would like to see. A very rough outline is to ferry to Santander, cross the Picos to Burgos and then pick up the headwaters of the Rio Ebro and follow it down to the Mediterranean coast near Tortosa. Also, now that we have enjoyed the experience of flying with the bikes, hopefully there will be physically no limit to where we can go. Who knows, if global warming becomes a reality, there is always Britain.